The Books of the Kingdom

Part 1—Samuel

Through the Bible
with Lance Lambert

The Books of the Kingdom

Part 1—Samuel

Through the Bible with
Lance Lambert

LANCE LAMBERT MINISTRIES

Richmond, Virginia, USA

ISBN: 978-1-68389-134-5

www.lancelambert.org

Contents

Unless otherwise indicated, Scripture quotations are from the American Standard Version 1901

Introduction

This book is part of a series Lance shared at Halford House in Richmond, Surrey, England in which he went through much of the Bible. Our desire is to make these and their accompanying study guides more readily available for reference and study.

At the date of this publication, this completes the first section of the Old Testament through Samuel. Ezra, Nehemiah and Esther are also available. Lance's teachings called, *How the Bible Came to Be,* begin our *Through the Bible* series. Lord willing, the rest of this series will be forthcoming!

As a part of what was originally known as the "Books of the Kingdom", Lance highlights how this book of Samuel is a pivotal point in Biblical history. Read on to see how Samuel is a link between the judges and the kings of Israel. May you be encouraged in the Lord through his ministry and kept until the day of His return as you meet Him in His Word!

With gratitude,
Lance Lambert Ministries team

1.
Saul and David— Kingship Principles

We come to the books of Samuel for our current study and the first problem we face is that in the Hebrew, the first and the second book of Samuel are one book. They are not looked upon as two books at all. It was only later, I think quite late in this age, that the division was made, and Samuel was divided into two books. In fact, as I think all of you will have noticed, if you look at the last chapter of the first book of Samuel and the first chapter of the second book, you will notice that there is no distinctive break at all in the narrative. These two books are one work.

Moreover, in the Septuagint version of the Old Testament, not only are I and II Samuel linked together, but also I and II Kings. They are all looked upon in the Septuagint version as one book in four sections. So, these are called the four books of the kingdom. If any of you have Knox's Version or if you look in the Septuagint Version, you will know that these are called the four books of the kingdom. It has been left out in the Revised, but in the Authorised Version, you will see a little subtitle to the title which says, "Or the first book of Kings," "I Samuel, or the first book of Kings." For example, "II Samuel, or the second book of Kings." Then similarly, "I Kings, or the third book of Kings." This straightaway gives us an understanding of these books to which we have now come.

The Kingdom Books—A History

The two books of Samuel and the two books of Kings are, in actual fact, a complete history of the kingdom. We have now come to a great point in Jewish history, and indeed, we have come to a very great point in the history of God's dealings with His own people, with His own children. For the first time, we are going to see a kingdom introduced. In I and II Samuel, and I and II Kings we have the complete history of that kingdom from its very inception in Samuel's day, right through to the Exile. The last chapters of II Kings bring us right up to the carrying away into exile. That was the end of the kingdom. After the Exile, there was no kingdom.

The kingdom ended when Judah was finally taken into exile. So, we really have got a complete history. If we look at these four books as a complete history of the kingdom, then I think we shall have a real understanding of what exactly the aim of the Lord is in giving them. There is going to come a point a bit later when we come to I and II Chronicles, when we are going to have to ask ourselves a very sensible question as to why on earth we should find another record going over exactly the same ground, and indeed including much of the same material. But that will wait until we come to it. These four are quite distinct from the first and second books of Chronicles. These four are a complete history, and they are written from a different standpoint than the two books of Chronicles. That is the first thing that we want to notice.

We have here a complete history of the kingdom. We have dealt with the history of the people settling in the land and inheriting it, what they really possessed of the land. We have dealt with Judges and the three appendices, including Ruth, dealing with the period of how what they left unpossessed became the ground for the enemy to bring the people into captivity and to worry the people all the time.

Intro to the Kingdom

Now, we have come to the introduction of the kingdom. We have come to a completely new phase in God's dealings with His people. We all know that the Bible is taken up completely with a progressive revelation which involves different phases. We have seen one great phase begin with Adam and end with Noah. We saw another phase which opened with Noah and ended with Abraham. Abraham was perhaps the greatest figure that we have come to study up to this point in Scripture. God's whole method with Abraham was entirely different from that with the others. He took Abraham in an entirely new way. You remember, He appeared to Abraham. He sovereignly extricated Abraham from a very, very cultured, heathen background and then took him out from it and did in him a very deep work which was to make him the father of a nation. Then we saw a new phase begin with Moses. We see now a new phase begin here.

Pre-natal History

We are at the beginning of the first book of Samuel. We are at the beginning of an entirely new phase in the history of the people of God, and we find that God has taken a great step forward. When the Lord took hold of Abraham, He took a great step forward, did He not? The history of humanity up to Abraham was general. The history following Abraham has been particular. It is bound up with a people. Before Abraham, it was just humanity. When He took Abraham, He was choosing a people. God took hold of Abraham with a people in view and all God's dealings with Abraham were of necessity, because from Abraham there was going to be produced a people.

So, we find that Abraham touches off the first great phase of the people of God. Up until then, history was general history. It was just to do with the nations. It was to do with the progress of the nations, the division of the nations, the allotment of the nations and so on. But when God took hold of Abraham, He took hold of one single man out of a certain family, in a certain people, in a certain nation. He took him away from it all into the desert, made him walk up and down in a land which he never owned, except for one little burial plot where he buried his own wife and he himself was later buried. That was all he ever owned in the land that God was to give him.

So that phase from Abraham to Joseph was a very necessary pre-natal history of the people of God. It was a long, drawn out, wearing, laborious history of inwrought principle. In Abraham, Isaac, and Jacob, God was to work out a principle in their lives so that from then on, these three would be the embodiment of all that God desired in a people. That is why God's dealings with

Abraham were different to His dealings with Isaac. His dealings with Jacob were different than with Abraham and Isaac. Each one of those three reveals to us something, some different aspect of what the Lord is after in a people.

That was the phase of pre-natal history, corporately. God was dealing with men, with a people in view. He took hold of one man. Then He took hold of a family that came out of that one man, and He dealt with them with a people in view. The people never came in their lifetime; Abraham never saw the people, and yet God was dealing with him in a long but sure and certain way to, in the end, produce a people. When Joseph goes into Egypt, some of the last developments of that phase are in the making. The Lord takes Joseph into Egypt to prepare the way for his brothers and his father, Jacob, to come into Egypt.

The Birth of a Nation

Then that phase ends in silence. A great period of history is passed over almost in silence. We do not know what has happened. The pre-natal history of the people of God is over. The next great phase begins with Moses and with Moses, God has a people. Moses does not have to look around for a people. Moses is already part of a nation, and the nation is in bondage. The nation has got to be redeemed. The nation has got to be delivered. A nation has got to be brought out. So, the next great phase begins in the history of the people of God, and that is the birth of a nation. The birth of a nation begins with the Passover and the Red Sea. That was the birth of a nation.

God in that day sovereignly put a sea between Egypt and His people. He delivered them in a miraculous way and in one single day, a nation was born. When the people landed on the other side of the Red Sea, they were an emancipated nation. In a day or two, they had left the house of bondage behind and they had become a nation. Then there is the great phase that is covered by Moses and Joshua and the book of Judges, and we could include many books when we consider Moses' books, could we not? Exodus, Leviticus, Numbers, Deuteronomy, and so on. All of that phase is a phase in which the nation is being brought into an understanding of its vocation as the dwelling place of God, as God's habitation and much else. That is a phase, as you know, of much revelation in every way, a tremendous amount of revelation.

Here was a nation. The nation comes out of Egypt in a very dispersed, scattered, and rebellious mood. The nation passes over under Joshua, as one man, into the land. Something has happened. Again, God's methods are long, they are laborious, but they are certain. A whole generation dies in the wilderness, but God takes up a new generation from out of a dying generation. That new generation was the generation that went over into the land to possess it.

Then you know that the book of Judges starts, as always, to prepare us for another new phase. It begins to show us all the weaknesses of the old phase and then begins to point us to the need of something which hitherto has not yet appeared on the scene.

Now, we have come to it. In I and II Samuel we have the beginning of a new phase. This is very, very important for us to understand. Samuel introduces a completely new phase or a new economy. He introduces a new phase of God's dealing.

Samuel – a Great Turning Point in the History of God's People

What is this new phase? The nation is going to be a kingdom. So, God unfolds to us something more in His thoughts. The people are not just to be so many people. They are to be welded and fused together into a kingdom and I and II Samuel are the beginning of that phase. Two new things come in with Samuel which were never there before. The first is the prophetic order, and the second is the monarchy. Let me put it this way. Many of you will say straightaway, "Oh, but there were prophets before Samuel," but Samuel is called in Scripture "the first of the prophets." The others that went before him, whilst they certainly did have a prophetic ministry (some of them), they were not prophets in the sense that those that succeeded Samuel were. Samuel was the first of a line of prophets. He was the last of the judges and the first of the prophets.

You see, up till then, prophecy had been a very spontaneous, and, I would say, a small ministry. It had not taken the place that it was now going to have. If we look at Scripture from the book of Samuel onwards, we shall find that the prophet was all-powerful. The prophet was so powerful, that in many ways in the people's minds, he ranked above the king. This is an altogether new movement of God. Samuel was the first of that line of prophets who introduced the kings, who anointed the kings, who, as it were, appointed the kings. The prophets were king-makers and king-breakers. They now became, in the hands of God, an instrument for correcting the king and the kingdom. They became an instrument in preserving the kingdom, warning the kingdom, and caring for it. This was something altogether new. We have had prophecy before now, yet we have never had a prophetic ministry of a type and an order which, as it were, is almost superior to the king himself.

Samuel was the beginning of this order, first of all in the way that he introduces Saul into the scene, then the way he instructs Saul, the way he anoints Saul, and the way he introduces Saul to the people. Then later on we see this order in the way that he contacts David, the way he anoints David, and the way he instructs David. Here for the first time, we have a new order altogether that we call the prophetic order. That is why there are two little terms in the book of Acts, one in chapter 13 and one in chapter three. One says, "until Samuel," and the other says, "from Samuel." Thus, we learn that Samuel is, as it were, a great turning point in the history of God's people.

We find two entirely new things come now into being which were never there before. The first is a long line of prophets that began with Samuel and ended with John the Baptist. The second is a long line of kings which began with David and ended with the Messiah. Samuel now was the one to introduce these two tremendous changes into God's economy: kingship and the prophetic order.

I think also we have to learn from the rather remarkable fact that from the earliest days, these two books were called the *Book of Samuel*, and now, more recently, the *Books of Samuel*. I do not know whether any of you have inquiring minds like mine. Have you never asked yourself why they are called the *Book of Samuel*? I have often asked myself when I was a little younger in the Lord, why on earth they were called the *Book of Samuel*. I was quite sure it had been a terrible mistake somewhere. I would have called them the *Book of David*. Why do you call them the *Book of Samuel*? There are only, at the very most, 15 chapters to do with Samuel—at the very most. Even that is not altogether to do with Samuel. Why then have these, from the earliest days, been called the *Book of Samuel* or recently the *Books of Samuel*? That is why it is so instructive. God tells us that He always begins a new phase with a man. Always, we have to understand that in the economy or the economies of God, He always begins with a man. The first started with Adam, of course, and then every new phase has been touched off by a man.

Now, shall we say, among the people of God there are three outstanding men. They are Abraham, Moses, and Samuel. Today, if you go to a modern orthodox Jew, he could tell you that the three greatest men in his history are Abraham, Moses, and Samuel. He will not tell you anything else. He will say that the three greatest men are Abraham, Moses, and Samuel, because these three men are men that introduced new phases in God's dealings with His people. That is why we do not find David, of all people, mentioned in the title. No, not in any shape or form or suggestion, is David mentioned here. If any name is given, and that from the earliest days, it is the name of Samuel. That is why Samuel is revered amongst the Jews.

Then again, we have to recognise that all these three men are pioneers. They are pioneers in a unique way—a way in which even such a man as Joshua was not. These men are absolutely pioneers. God did with each one a remarkable thing. With each of these three men is a new beginning and each begins in the sovereignty of God. Each of the three men that touch off a new phase in God's dealings with men begin with God's sovereignty and grace.

Why did God choose Abraham? Abraham did not do a thing, yet God appeared unto Abraham. It is not recorded that Abraham sought the Lord. It is not recorded that Abraham called upon the Lord. It is not recorded that Abraham followed after the Lord. It does say the God of glory appeared unto our father Abraham. He laid hold of Abraham. Moses was exactly the same. God from the very beginning, in a sovereign way, preserved Moses. In the same way from before his birth, Samuel had all the marks of the sovereignty of God. Here we learn once more one of the great principles of God in any new phase, whether it be in our days or whether it be right back in Old Testament days. Whenever God is going to do a new thing, it always begins with His sovereignty. Always. It always begins with the sovereignty of God. This is one of the most remarkable things you will find in Scripture, but it is all the way through. When God touches off a completely new phase in His economy, it always begins with His own initiation, His own sovereignty.

We have already mentioned that Samuel is the last of the judges and the first of the prophets. Samuel combines in himself all the Old Testament offices. He is a priest, he is a prophet, and he is a judge. He combines priesthood, prophecy, and rulership or kingship in himself. These three offices are combined in one person.

Another thing about Samuel is that he is a Levite, and he is a Nazirite. All these different things are woven together in one man. He combines everything and he becomes the great turning point in Jewish history when the nation, as it were, moved from one phase of a more democratic government right over into a monarchy. There Samuel stands at the heart of it all as God's instrument.

Another interesting thing is that Samuel had influence. I want to underline this fact because I think Samuel is forgotten by Christians today. His is a name that is not mentioned so often. Whereas in actual fact, if you look through Scripture, you will find it gives Samuel a tremendous place. Samuel influenced the nation for generations to come, as I suppose no other man has influenced it, except, of course, Abraham and Moses. His influence outlived his death by generations.

For instance, Samuel was the man who instituted the schools of the prophets. Now let us get this absolutely clear. The schools of the prophets were not Bible colleges as so many people seem to think. They always seem to refer to these schools of the prophets as if they were Bible colleges. These schools of the prophets were more akin to our universities. They were centres where the young men of the land were taught to read and to write, and then they were taught the law of God and, as it were, out from that everything developed. These were the schools of the prophets which Samuel instituted, which were to become one of the greatest institutions of Israel.

This is all an aside, but do you know that, speaking from a human standpoint, we probably would never have had the Scriptures which we have if it had not been for the schools of the prophets? This is where students took these scriptures and carefully scribed them, copied them, made many different manuscripts of the one, and stored them in the different centres of the land. The centres of the prophets became, as it were, centres of education and culture. If you read a Jewish history, you will find that Samuel is looked upon as one of the greatest statesmen of Jewish history, because he paved the way for the kingdom, not only spiritually, but culturally and educationally. He paved the way for the kingdom.

Samuel was the one who was to lay a foundation which still existed in the days of our Lord. He was the one who was to put the Jew on an entirely new footing educationally with the nations roundabout, so that to this day, the Jew is known as a bookworm. We very rarely find that Jews will excel in sport or in other things like that. They excel in the realm of literature and art. Samuel was the one that converted the nation into a nation of bookworms. So we see that in the Lord's day, to uncover one's body was considered to be sinful, and still is amongst orthodox Jews. But to study any form of writing is considered to be almost sacred.

This all began in a simple way with Samuel and his institution of the school of the prophets. So let us forget the business about Bible colleges and so on for a while, and remember that they were more centres of learning, where the young of the nation were brought in and were taught to read and taught to write, and then taught to understand something of the history and the heritage of their people. We have to confess that the schools of the prophets did not do much else. Educationally and culturally, they did a lot, but whenever God wanted someone to do something, He never looked for them in the schools of the prophets. He always took them, as it were, from 'nowhere.' Think of a man like Elijah. He never gave them schools of the prophets, although much of his life later on was spent in helping the prophets and so on.

Yet he himself was a very rough, shepherd-like character that was brought from out of Gilead. So, we could go on mentioning other characters, but the Lord bypassed the school for the prophets in that way, as I am afraid often He does today. He still always maintains His sovereignty in the way in which He raises up men and women to be those that are instruments in His hand. So, we want to at least recognise together that Samuel was a most remarkable man.

We have seen already in our previous study on Ruth, the Lord working sovereignly to provide a king. Right in the midst of all that darkness and carnage and evil, in the days of the book of Judges, the Lord is working to provide a king. He does not work apart from it; He works with it. Is this not always like the Lord? He always takes failure. Where we fail, that is the point in which He starts to recover. He takes the Moabitess. He takes people who failed because they have moved off God's ground and gone into backsliding and gone into a foreign country. All those things which were just evidence of failure and compromise and breakdown, God takes *that*, and from *that* point He provides a king. So, the book of Ruth ends with a king.

Now, we must go back a little. We have already had the veil drawn aside and we have seen that a king has been provided. Here then we find the instrument which God is raising up to introduce this kingship and we begin with the books of Samuel. Now, because the different sections of these books overlap, we shall look at the first 16 chapters and then next we shall go back again over the last chapters from about chapter 8.

Authorship and Date

Now, a word on the authorship and the date of this book of Samuel. The author is not clearly indicated at all. It is obviously a compilation. It has been compiled from various documents, and that is quite clear if we look together at the book. Turn with me to I Samuel 10:25:

> *Then Samuel told the people the manner of the kingdom, and wrote it in a book, and laid it up before Jehovah. And Samuel sent all the people away, every man to his house.*

So, we understand that here we have reference to a certain document written by Samuel himself. Now, turn to I Chronicles 29:29:

> *Now the acts of David the king, first and last, behold, they are written in the history of Samuel the seer, and in the history of Nathan the prophet, and in the history of Gad the seer ...*

So evidently, we have three more documents. Or possibly the one concerning Samuel is the same that we have already seen mentioned. We have a history of Samuel, a history written by Nathan, and a history written by Gad. Then, look at II Samuel 1:18:

> *(and he bade them teach the children of Judah the song of the bow: behold, it is written in the book of Jashar):*

So, we have there another document. It is quite obvious that the book of Samuel is a compilation made from various documents. There are one or two theories that have been put forward, but I think that it would be quite true and accurate to say that the book of Samuel is probably, very largely, the work of Samuel, Nathan and Gad. Probably the first 24 chapters, at any rate, are by the hand of Samuel and the rest by Nathan and Gad.

I think you will probably all know that Nathan and Gad were intimately associated with David. You remember it was Nathan the prophet who went in and rebuked David for his sin over Uriah the Hittite. Also, you will remember that it was Gad the prophet, who interpreted to David the plague because he numbered the people. These prophets were intimately associated with David in the kingdom. So, it would seem that this would explain how the book of Samuel could be written, obviously from an eyewitness account, and yet at the same time have the marks of being written a good deal later than the events recorded. That is why these books particularly have become the centre of so much controversy in this question on liberalism in the word of God. It is simply that it is probable that the three or more documents used were written by eyewitnesses of the events and have been compiled together by a scribe at a later date.

Another thing that we might say is that this book of Samuel covers a period of approximately one hundred years. It covers from the death of Samson, the beginning of Eli, more or less, right over to the accession of Solomon to the throne. That is quite a big period of a hundred years, approximately a century. It was probably written in its present form, or compiled in the form in which we now have it, during the reign of Rehoboam, the first king of Judah. You remember that at Solomon's death, Israel was split into two, into Israel and Judah. It was probably compiled in the form in which we have it now in that reign. The reason being (if you want to have any evidence for it) is that first of all it speaks of David's death. Secondly, in at least one place, it speaks of the kings of Judah, which would be unheard of before the division of Israel into Israel and Judah. So, we would say that it was written not before the death of David and not before the division of Israel into two. That means it would probably have been written then in the reign of Rehoboam. It is also possible that Nathan and Gad, who certainly outlived David, may well have lived on into the reign of Rehoboam. There is a possibility of that if you look into the history itself.

The Key

What is the key to the book of Samuel? Well, I do not think we need to spend very long on what is the key. I expect most of you already know it. The key is quite obvious, much more obvious than in some of the books—it is kingship—twofold. It is the king (kingship) and the kingdom. That is the key to this book.

We find everything is explained by kingship in the book of Samuel. It is revealed negatively in Saul and then positively in David. That is why you will find that Saul is included in the account, although he was not really God's king at all. He is included in the account because it reveals to us what is not kingship according to God and what can never attain to real kingship under the hand of God, whereas David is the exact opposite. It reveals to us, in spite of the obvious, quite obvious failings and waywardness of the man, it reveals to us what can be brought under the hand of God to the throne.

It is interesting to note that in these four books (I and II Samuel and I and II Kings), we are not given a strictly chronological order of events. This again is a thing that puzzles many people. But as always in the Bible, the aim governs the scope. We have said that so many times in our Bible study series, and yet it is so important to an understanding of the word of God. The aim governs the scope. It is not a strictly chronological order of events. That is why you will find, first of all, we deal with Samuel when he is a boy, a little boy, and then suddenly his whole life is almost passed over until we find him an old, grey-haired man at the end of his life. Then we dwell for some time upon his end. In the same way, Saul is introduced as a young man, an unmarried young man, in his father's house. Then suddenly, there is a whole portion of his life left out, and we suddenly find that he is forty or thereabouts when next we find him.

Then again, you cannot even say that the book of Samuel is pure biography. It is not pure biography. There is much that we would include in a biography that is not included here. That is why people who have written biographies of Samuel and David and so on have found themselves hard put to fill quite a few large gaps in their lives. This is not pure biography in the same way that it is not pure chronological history.

The aim of these books is to introduce the kingdom of God under the guidance of the word of God. That is why the last four chapters of the second book of Samuel are not history at all, like the last few chapters of Judges and Ruth. They go back over what has been narrated and insert one or two incidents as a kind of appendix which reveals two or three things. The idea of the last four chapters of the second book of Samuel is to show to us finally that the kingdom has been truly established. It tells us the mighty men that have come who took part in its establishment. Then it shows to us how the kingdom of God for the first time was absolutely under the guidance of the word of God through the prophet. The word of God did not come through the king. The word of God came through the prophet. This was a new thought altogether that there should be leadership on one side, wedded with prophecy, the word of God, on the other.

That, I say, is the aim of these four books that comprise this history of the kingdom, to show to us the kingdom of God under the word of God, in the same way that we today have exactly the same position. We are in the kingdom of God and we are under the guidance of the word of God. So, we can learn a tremendous amount from these chapters. We have got to hear the word of God as something that can correct us and must correct us, rebuke us because we must be rebuked, encourage us because we must be encouraged, comfort us because we must be comforted. That is the whole function of the word of God, to build us up and to keep us in the way, and by God's grace, to bring us to full attainment of all that God has given to us in Christ.

Pointing to the King

We can see, therefore, that if the key to this book is kingship and the kingdom, we can look at the book of Samuel in one or two ways. First of all, we can look upon it as David's prefiguring [foreshadowing] of God's king. I think you all know just the remarkable way in which David does foreshadow the coming of the Lord. He himself, as it were, did not know it fully and yet, you see it from his Psalms. In Psalm 22 and other Psalms like that, we find that words are put into his mouth, wrung out of bitter, agonising experience, which were later to be taken up by the Lord Himself in the most sombre and solemn part of His death. "My God, my God, why hast Thou forsaken me?" Yet you see, here the Lord took hold of a man a thousand years before the Lord Jesus should appear, and put him into such a way, led him into such circumstances, brought him into such situations that He was able to wring out of him, as it were, that which absolutely prefigured the Lord in His deepest and most terrible agony.

We can look at many of David's psalms, and when you think of David's word, "My own familiar friend has lifted up his heel against me," and many other psalms like that, we see they were not written cheaply. They were not written superficially. They did not just come out of a kind of poetic, artistic type of mind or attitude. They were wrung out of his heart experience of life and of humanity and of God. Because of that, you find that without hardly knowing it, David prefigures and foreshadows the Lord Himself in his own way and life. So, we can take the key to this book, which is kingship, and we can look at David as a type of the Lord Jesus, and a very, very wonderful type indeed, and learn from that.

Although one has to be awfully careful about this sometimes, I think in the way that some saints foreshadowed the Lord, we, in this age, can express the Lord. We have to be very careful about saying that. But I have often thought of it, and it has often comforted me, to think that as saints hundreds of years before the Lord were put into circumstances in which they prefigured their Lord, so we are put into circumstances and situations. In the same way, we are writing history. Well, of course, that is not very easy for you or me to think of in our insignificant surroundings and so on, but nevertheless, it is true that we are writing history. I have no doubt about it that the book of Acts will be a continued story. When we get to glory, we shall probably find that the whole thing has been written so there will be a counterpart of this New Testament age to all that we have in the word of God. For after all, the word of the Lord abideth forever. I do not believe that the New Testament age is going to be passed over in silence at all. I am quite sure that we are going to find that the "through faith" chapter is going to be expanded to include quite a few other events and incidents. In the same way we shall find in the glory one day that many of us, in the simplest, most humble surroundings, like Hannah, like Ruth, like Mary, and like Elizabeth by God's grace and in His sovereignty became the ground for instruction for principalities and powers, for those things that watch, those things that look on. Without our hardly knowing it, only dimly seeing it, we have become, as it were, a veritable instruction to those principalities and powers.

Well, there is something very, very wonderful about looking at it from that point of view. I think we can also look at it from another point of view as well. We can look upon it as the *kingdom of God*. We mean by that, not just simply God's king, but God's kingdom with its government, its administration, its centre, its home, its life, its everything. You know, God's kingdom is just like that. It all is involved in the person, God's king.

But out from God's king there is a government, there is a cabinet, there is an administration, then there is a life. It is all there in God's kingdom. We can view these chapters in the same way. God's king is not just a detached, ethereal, sentimental figurehead. You do not believe that the Lord Jesus is going to be very much like royalty today, do you? Will He be a sentimental figurehead, a heart which sentimentally draws people together? Do you believe that? No, I believe that the Lord Jesus is not just a figurehead, that sentimentally draws His people together. He is Himself head over all things. He has a government and an administration. He has a kingdom in which His word is absolutely all-powerful and authoritative. That is the kingdom.

When you and I are brought into relationship with the Lord Jesus, we enter the kingdom of God by birth. That is something which is very, very wonderful. In the days to come, of course, when God has got His government, His administration perfected, then we are going to see its outworking in the universe. Then there will be territories to be governed, and there will be vast domains and realms brought under the government of a people who have been perfected into the likeness of their king.

So, we can look at this book of Samuel in that light. We can look upon it as the light of the establishment of a kingdom. Then we can look upon it, and this is very important, as revealing to us principles of kingship. For God has made us all royal sons and daughters. The whole point of His house and of His schooling is to train us in the principle of kingship. Adam was told to have dominion. And all down through the different ages, God has been seeking to instruct us in the principles of dominion.

The Coming Kingdom

In the same way, we make a big mistake if we think that this life is everything. This life is like the cave of Adullam. One day we are coming out to take the kingdom. There is coming a day when we are going to come out as a people wedded together, built together, fused together into a solid home, one solid unit, a head and a body. In that day, the kingdom will be taken and the King of kings will be crowned. That is what this life is. That is why sometimes it is so very dark and so very gloomy. That is why it is so very shut in. That is why it is so very restricted. That is why we are put with people, some of whom we cannot get on with, but we have to get on with them, and we have got to be built in with them. That is the whole history of the kingdom of God. What is it? It is kingship being learned. It is the principles of kingship being, as it were, inwrought.

That is how we can look upon this book. We have been made kings and priests unto God. It is not enough for us to be ruled over. God, by developing a Christ-like moral stature and character, will make us kings. He is not content to have, as it were, just slaves that bow to Him. He would so develop us, so train us that we become kings because of something inside. It is not, as so many people think, that one day we are all going to have golden crowns placed upon our heads and that then there is going to be a cry, "Long live the king!" or something like that. It is not that everyone is going to say, "Now, look, here is King Lance and here is king somebody else and here is king somebody else." That is not the thought of Scripture, although many of our hymns suggest it, that we are going to be crowned like that. Well, no doubt there is coming something along that line of a public recognition. But how will it come?

No man and no woman in the kingdom of God will ever be given kingship who has not got kingship inside. The old word in the book of Proverbs we often quote, "a man's gift makes room for him," is as true in heaven as it is down here. Let me put it this way: if in heaven there is something of moral stature, of moral character, of Christ Himself reproduced in character and moral quality and backbone, that man, that woman, of necessity, will be in God's administration. That is how it works out and that is how we can look at the book of Samuel. We can look upon it as a book of the principles of kingship—kingship principles.

Kingship Principles

How did David come to the throne? Why did Saul fall from the throne? Why was Saul cut off from the throne and why was David kept on the throne? Can you tell me anywhere where Saul murdered a man and took his wife? You will not find this anywhere. You cannot find it. Now tell me, can you find anywhere in the book of Samuel where Saul numbered the people in disobedience to God? Then, for that reason, the terrible plague hit the people of God? Can you find it?

Can you find anywhere in the Scripture other things like qualities of humility in Saul? Now, you may say to me, "No, I cannot find any humility about Saul." But I can. I can prove to you from Scripture that, naturally speaking, Saul was quite humble when they tried to crown him. He hid in the baggage and he had to be dragged out. He would not be crowned. When first he was told that he was to be king, he said that he was the least, and his father's house was the least, and his tribe was the least. Why choose him?

You know, another time, there were some other nasty people who did not like Saul's being king and refused to give a gift and refused to acknowledge it. When Saul led the people into victory against the Philistines, the people came and said, "Now, please, we want to put to death the people that would not recognise you." But Saul said, "No, this is the day of victory. No man shall die." He saved the lives. He seemed to be a very generous man. I could tell you all kinds of things about Saul which were exceedingly generous. Now tell me, why did Saul not come to the throne of God and why is it that David did?

In the answer to those questions, you will find the principles of kingship. Why it is that so many good, natural qualities do not qualify us, and why it is that a man with so many very real sins could be qualified? In that, you find the principles of kingship. In Saul, it is negative. All that is good about him and all that is bad, and yet, a divine veto. But in David, we find all that is good about him and all that is bad about him, but divine acceptance. Now, why? You see, we can look at this book and the key to it is the kingdom or kingship. We can look at this book as revealing to us principles of kingship: the way we come to serve. In so doing, we shall find the answer to much else.

The House of God

I just want you also to note that the house of God is hidden in the first chapters. Mind you, a tremendous amount happens around the house of God. The very opening chapters of Samuel are found within the tabernacle—at Shiloh. From then on, we find everything has been brought back to the tabernacle. However, the thing I want you to notice is that although kingship and the kingdom are the key to the book of Samuel, you will find at the very end that it has all got a greater purpose than even that. You find the last chapter of the second book of Samuel ends with the purchase, very insignificant, the purchase of a threshing floor and the raising of an altar. Why mention that? Because that threshing floor is to become the site of the house of God. I never find anywhere any concern or yearning whatsoever in Saul for the house of God, but I find in David, from his earliest days, before ever kingship entered his mind, a passionate love for the house of God—passionate.

If, as we believe, Psalm 23 was written in the very earliest days of David's life when he was still a shepherd lad, it may well be that from those earliest days, the passion of his heart and life was the house of God. We can certainly know it was later by his Psalms and by the record of this book. We are shown, as time goes on, something hidden at the beginning begins to be unfolded at the end. We suddenly discover that this man's heart is not on the throne at all. It is upon God's habitation. That is why the closing years of his life were spent in gathering together material for the building and the construction of the house of God. That is why David's whole concern at the end was to instruct Solomon, his son, in how to build the house. It was his concern. It was his passion. It was the one object of his heart. I think that what perhaps broke his heart was the fact that he was not able to build it himself. He was rejected from doing that by the Lord in God's sovereignty. But nevertheless, that was his passion. We do not find this passion in Saul. We do find it in David. Saul is different. There is something there which is a key, I think, to much more. David, from the beginning, had his heart set on the house of God.

Some of us wonder from whom David first learned about the house of God. Tradition tells us, the rabbis tell us, that David's father, Jesse, was by profession the veil-weaver of the temple. It may have been from Jesse or his mother that David learnt his first lessons in the house of God. But others of us think that it might have been Samuel who first taught David the great need of God's habitation. I am sure that somehow or another, David owed much to Samuel.

So, we find here through this book of Samuel, whilst the key to it is kingship and the kingdom, we are going to find that it leads to God's habitation. We are going to find that the climax of it all is found in Solomon. The house of God is finally built and dedicated, and the glory of God fills it.

2.
The Instrument to Introduce the Kingdom

Review

As you will remember, in the Hebrew these two books of Samuel are one book. They were divided into two sections, and in fact, with the first and second book of Kings, were looked upon as four sections of one work. That is, it is a complete history of the kingdom in four sections. It was only, I believe, in 1570 that it was finally divided into what we have now, so that it became the first and the second book of Samuel.

We have now reached the third great phase of God's dealings with His people. There are three distinct phases in the Old Testament that we have seen so far. There is going to be a fourth phase, which we shall come to in another study, but there are three distinct phases in God's dealings with His people.

The first began with Abraham. Until Abraham God dealt with individuals, He dealt with the world and humanity in a general way, but when He took Abraham, it was in a particular way. God sovereignly chose Abraham out of many, and Abraham was the beginning of a new phase in God's economy. We get that phase which we call the pre-natal history of the people of God, running from Abraham right the way down into Egypt until the time of Joseph. That was one great phase in God's dealings with His people. In that time, He hammered out principle. He hammered out a pre-natal history. He got something very precious in those days.

Then, the next great phase began with the actual birth of a nation, the birth of the people of God. Again, as always with every new phase in God's economy, we find a man. As it was Abraham in the first, it was Moses in the second. Then that phase carries us right through to the present one. It is a phase that lasts from Moses to Samuel. It is, as you know, the story of the elementary dealings of God with His people.

Now we come to these two books of Samuel, and we are once again at the beginning of a new phase in God's economy. This phase we call the kingdom.

As we have gone through the books of the Old Testament so far, we have found that each one has carried us a step forward. Each book has been a distinct and decisive step forward in God's revelation of His thought and purpose to us. Now we come for the first time to an altogether new concept. This concept, this idea, this thought has never before been defined or expressed or stated. It is the kingdom. You and I know how much of the New Testament is taken up with the kingdom. So for the first time in the Bible, we are moving into the phase of the kingdom of God. We have already found something of God's election in the days of Abraham. We have found something of redemption and the house of God in the days of Moses. We found something of the land and its settling in the days of Joshua. Now we have come to Samuel, and it is very expressive and instructive that the name of Samuel should be given to this particular phase of God's dealings. This is a very wonderful thing because, in fact, if you read the two books of Samuel, you will find that they deal very little with Samuel. Yet it is Samuel's name that is given to this particular record. That is not necessarily because Samuel wrote it. If he did write it, he could have only written the first 24 chapters at the very most of the first book of Samuel.

We believe it has been given to him because Samuel was the man who gave the kingdom its character. He was, as you know, one of the great turning points in the history of God's people. He combined in himself all three offices. He was a prophet. He was the first of the great line of prophets. He was a priest and he was a judge. He combined these three great offices of the Old Testament into himself. He was not only that, but he was also a Levite and a Nazirite in one. He combined everything together in one man and you know that he was the man who was to influence Israel for generations to come in a multitude of ways. Particularly, of course, in his instituting of the schools of the prophets which were to affect the country so deeply, educationally, and culturally, and also spiritually. So, we find that Samuel is a remarkable man, a man who is not given the place that he should be given by the people of God. Samuel is a man often overlooked, but in fact he is amongst the three great men of the Old Testament: Abraham, Moses, and Samuel.

Remember also, that there are two altogether new things that now are introduced at this point in the Bible. The first is the monarchy or kingship or the kingdom, and the second is the word of God by prophecy. We, of course, have already seen prophets in the Bible. Moses was a prophet and there have been other prophets. Deborah was a prophetess, and there were others who prophesied before the Lord. But we have not yet found the prophets of the line of which Samuel was the first. For instance, later on we begin to find a ministry, a clearly defined prophetic ministry. Consider the book of Isaiah. Samuel was the first of a long line of prophets that was to be terminated with John the Baptist.

He was the first of those prophets, of the men who brought God's word in a very definite way to His people. It is instructive to note that in the books of Samuel and Kings many of the more outstanding miracles of the period of the Passover and of the wilderness and of the going into the land have now quietly, quietly faded into the background. Now we find that kingship takes its place and also the word of God by God's vessels.

We do not now find angels so much in evidence as they were before, nor the more definitely supernatural forms of speaking and visiting of the people of God. Instead, now we find that God speaks through men, carefully chosen, carefully prepared, and appointed.

The Key to the Book

We found that the key to the first and second book of Samuel is simply kingship. That is the key to this book. As we move through it, we shall find that from whatever angle we look at it, it is kingship and the kingdom—God's king and God's kingdom—that is now really in view.

We have already noted a rather remarkable method of the author in contrasting people. He contrasts Peninnah and Hannah, Eli and Samuel, Saul and David, and Jonathan and the 400 in the cave of Adullam. All the way through, he is contrasting and comparing people—a person, with a person. This is one of his rather remarkable methods, which is in itself a very interesting study.

The Instrument

The first thing that you will notice is that these chapters in our outline overlap. The first thing that you will note in the first 16 chapters of the first book is what we have called the instrument to bring in God's kingdom. Here we have the preparation of the instrument that is to be used to introduce not only the king, but the kingdom. It is always instructive in the word of God to see the diligent care and forethought and planning of God before ever any real new thought is introduced.

God is always a slow worker, but a sure worker. It is most interesting to find in these different phases of God's dealings with His people, how He works hiddenly, slowly but surely, to achieve His end. Here we have such an instance. The first thing we find in the first three chapters is the producing of that instrument. Now I want you to note this very carefully, because in many ways the word of God seems to give a real emphasis to Samuel's birth and Samuel's upbringing, more so in some ways than it does to greater characters in the story.

Prepared in an Evil Day

You will note that it was a time of evil days. You have only to read through the second and third chapters of Samuel and you will find how evil the days were in which God worked to provide Samuel. Eli's two sons were evil men. They were not just evil in the sense that they were teaching error or that they were compromised men. They were utterly immoral, and they used the house of God as a means to satisfy themselves in every way. It was not merely that when the offerings of God were brought to the house they took what belonged to God for themselves. It says they took the best before ever the offerors had a chance to offer to God what was His. The priests took it straightaway. But it also says that they committed immorality within the very precincts of the tabernacle.

This was the atmosphere of the days of Samuel. This lad was brought up in such a poisoned and perverted atmosphere. It was not merely that it was a miracle that God provided Samuel. You realise that it was a miracle that Samuel was ever kept true to God, since it was at the very, very early age of three that he was taken into the house of God and reared by Eli in the very presence of these evil men. Eli's two sons, Hophni and Phineas, were known throughout Israel for their evil ways. They caused the worship of God and the service of God to be spoken of in a very evil way. That is the background.

However, as always, that background, whilst it is absolutely in keeping with the book of Judges, is the theme of God's working to recovery. This is always God's method. God does not work in a detached way. He always works in the midst of the failure. Therefore, in the very midst of this failure we find two people, Elkanah and Hannah. Elkanah means "God acquired," and Hannah means "favour."

Hannah

These were to be the father and the mother of Samuel. They evidently had a history with the Lord. If you read the first chapter of Samuel, you will find there is a history there in Elkanah and Hannah. They spoke together about the Lord. There was failure in the house. It has been suggested that because Hannah was barren, Elkanah took a second wife. His second wife had many children. This was the scene of continual strife and misery within the household of Elkanah. Peninnah evidently provoked Hannah as much as she possibly could by inferring and implying all kinds of things. There is nothing like living in the atmosphere of superiority. There is nothing like living in the atmosphere of someone who is satisfied and content when you have nothing.

This was the way that Peninnah provoked Hannah. There was a history of suffering and a travail in the background, and it came to a head each year when they went up to the tabernacle, to the sacrifice, to the yearly festival. It says here quite clearly that it came to such an impasse that Hannah could not sit down and eat whilst the rest were eating at the festival.

Hannah was so filled with bitterness of soul, that all she could do was just rush out. She found her way into the tabernacle and there she began to pour out the bitterness of her heart. So obviously filled with agony and so in travail was this woman that she was like someone that was drunk. Her lips moved, but no voice was audible. Do you remember that Eli thought that she was drunk?

Yet in the midst of this suffering, an attitude was forged. Now, suffering can either embitter us and make us sour and difficult and awkward people, or it can forge an attitude of devotion to the Lord. In Hannah's case, she was not embittered and rebellious against the Lord, full of questions: "Why doesn't the Lord answer me? Why doesn't the Lord provide? Why doesn't He do it? How can He let Peninnah, that wicked woman, provoke me all the time? Why does He bless the person who is not devoted to the Lord and leaves me unblessed?" No. If she had these questions, Hannah got through the lot and her attitude was one of utter devotion to the Lord. She said, "If the Lord gives me a child, a son, I will give him back to the Lord all the days of his life."

Now, that was no light-hearted vow. For if Hannah's one great passion was to have a son, then obviously to give him back into the temple of the Lord and rarely see him again was not going to satisfy her very much. I am quite sure that Hannah was not interested in the pain and travail connected with the birth of a son—to see his end, to see his back for the rest of his days, rarely to touch him again, never to see him grow up, never to have any hand in his education and instruction. I cannot believe that is so. It reveals an attitude. Hannah was a woman of spiritual insight and foresight. It is quite obvious that she saw the evil of the days around her. She recognised the need and there came a point when in her suffering she got to a place of absolute acquiescence and harmony with the Lord. It did not mean that she did not suffer. It meant that she suffered all the more, but she was in the place of harmony with the Lord. She had a peace, evidently, that was deeper than the bitterness of her soul.

Now, here is the interesting thing: twice in the record it says clearly that the Lord shut up her womb. It is definitely stated that the Lord took the action. Why did He treat Hannah in this way? Because the Lord was bringing Hannah into a union with Himself. He was engineering the circumstances, manoeuvring everything around to bring Hannah into the place where she had an insight and a knowledge of the Lord, which Peninnah, with all her children, could never have. Peninnah had her children. She had household duties. She had a husband. I do not suppose she had very much time to think with all her children.

But Hannah was kept barren in order that she might be able to reflect and meditate and in her very yearning and concern, I think she came to a conclusion that we shall find came out in the end when she gave Samuel back to the Lord. Out of that attitude, Samuel was born. When the Lord got the attitude, Samuel was given, and we find that a new phase in God's economy begins.

A New Phase in God's Economy

You will note something else, too. Samuel was wholly given from his birth. I am going to read to you from a literal version by Edersheim [see Edersheim's *Israel under Samuel, Saul, and David, to the birth of Solomon* p. 7–8] because we do not have the real play on words. May I just say this? Hannah was not a simple ignoramus, as many people think she was. They think she was a simple peasant woman. Hannah was a woman of real and obvious intelligence and culture. The way that her heart burst that into song is something tremendous. You, of course, all realise that Hannah's song is the basis of Mary's song. Mary took up Hannah's song and enlarged it.

This is what she says in 1 Samuel 1 verses 27–28:

For this boy have I prayed; and [the Lord] gave me my
asking which I asked of Him. And now I (on my part)
make him the asked one unto [the Lord] all the days
that he lives: he is 'the asked one' unto [the Lord]!

She was using the word *ask* in Hebrew and she played upon it and her whole thought in verse 27 and 28 was simply this: "I asked the Lord for a son. He has asked me for him. God has a need; I have a need. We both brought our need together. God's need was met by me, and my need was met by God." She played upon the words. Samuel means "heard of the Lord."

So she said: I have given him back to the Lord. I asked him of the Lord. The Lord heard my asking and gave me the asked one of the Lord. So, I give him back to the Lord because He has asked for him. That really is the circumstance of the birth of Samuel. There was a history there. There was something behind his birth and there was something in his birth.

Furthermore, you will note that his service began with the burnt offering. Samuel's life of service began with the offering of a bullock, a burnt offering. This was to symbolise Samuel. From the very beginning, Samuel would be consumed by the Lord. There was nothing about Samuel's life or being that was, in any way, to be given to any other. He was wholly for the Lord. Samuel's life can be symbolised in the burnt offering, which his father and mother offered when they dedicated him to the Lord. So we find that Samuel, at the age of three, enters the service of God, a very young age to begin in the service of God. But at the age of three we find him in the house of God.

The Development of Samuel

I then want you to notice how God develops a ministry. From chapter three, verse 19 to chapter eight, you find a development of this instrument. God begins to develop him. It is amazing how Samuel could have maintained such a sensitiveness to the Lord in an atmosphere of compromise and luxury and comfort. Yet he maintained that sensitivity to the Lord right the way through. He never lost it. First, He develops him by an experience of defeat.

The Word of God by Samuel

It says clearly that the word of God came by Samuel. In 1 Samuel 3:1 it says that the word of the Lord was rare in those days. There was no frequent vision or there was no open vision. Then it says,

> And Samuel grew, and the Lord was with him, and did let none of his words fall to the ground. And all Israel from Dan even to Beer-sheba knew that Samuel was established to be a prophet of the Lord. And the Lord appeared again in Shiloh; for the Lord revealed himself to Samuel in Shiloh by the word of the Lord. And the word of Samuel came to all Israel (vv 19–20).

So, we find that Samuel studied the word of the Lord and as he studied the word of the Lord, the Lord came to him. The Lord appeared once again in the tabernacle. There were the first stirrings of a new beginning with God.

The Ark Captured

But as always, we find that the Lord allows things to get right down to the very bottom before a reformation ever begins. In the next chapter, we find that the ark is captured. You know the story. The children of Israel went out to battle and were defeated, and so they decided to take the ark out into battle. But when they took the ark out into battle, the Philistines fought and they took the ark. And you know the awful and sad result of the ark's being taken. Even though Eli was a compromised man when he was told that his two sons were dead, that was not the thing that killed him, yet when he heard that the ark of God was captured, he fell off the seat and broke his neck.

Then you know how the story goes on about his daughter-in-law. She gave birth to her child. She was so heartbroken, not so much over the death of her husband as over the fact that the ark had been captured, that she called the son Ichabod, "No glory." That is the sad, despairing note of gloom that has settled upon the beginning of Samuel's ministry. The ark, for the first time, has gone into captivity. Eli is dead through shock, his two sons slain with the ark. His daughter-in-law died in childbirth, and the Philistines in control.

The Ark Among the Philistines

However, here is the beginning of Samuel's instruction. The Philistines put the ark in the temple of Dagon. They put it before Dagon. There is no man there. They just put the ark of

God in the temple of Dagon. The next morning, they find that Dagon has fallen off his foundation and is flat on his face before the ark. So, they pitch him back up again and put him into place, evidently feeling that some mistake had occurred, not connecting it with the ark. But the next morning, they find that Dagon has fallen down, his head is broken off, and his arms are broken off and it says, in a rather wry way, "only the stump of Dagon was left to him."

They then decided that it was time, to move the ark out of the temple of Dagon. They moved the ark out of the temple of Dagon and in each city where they brought the ark, there was a plague. We believe today it was the bubonic plague. In bubonic plague, you get swelling of the groins and with awful boils. As this plague spread from city to city, wherever they took the ark, so the plague spread. They began to connect the two things together, and the Philistines became exceedingly worried. They found they had got something too hot to hold in their midst. It was not that they were dealing with people. They were not dealing with flesh and blood. They were dealing with the presence of God. The presence of God was symbolised by the ark. This was the outward evidence of the presence of God. God was well able to take care of His ark. He needed no man to put forth his hand and steady the ark. The Lord was quite able to make Himself so unwanted and unnecessary to the enemies of God that they would send back the ark into the land. This was all Samuel's instruction.

The Beginning of Samuel's Reformation

Samuel began to learn one of his greatest lessons. God is able to take care of Himself. God's work does not need our help.

God's work God carries on. God undertakes responsibility for His work. If it is His work, if it is according to His mind, God is responsible for it. He does not need anyone else to go running after the ark to bring it back. He can take care of the ark. He can make the ark an embarrassment in the hands of the enemies and in the presence of their gods. This is exactly what He does, and this was His instruction to Samuel.

Samuel had seen what compromise in the high priest, and evil and sinfulness in the priest's sons had done for the house of God. He had seen where it had ended—tragedy, gloom, and despair. Now, in the darkest days of Samuel's memory, he begins to learn his deepest lessons in the sovereignty of God.

Now, it is very interesting that after a while the Philistines bring all their diviners, soothsayers, and witches together and ask of them what they should do about the ark. When they besought their spirits, and so on, they got the answer: you must make a trespass offering. This trespass offering was to be images of the boils and images of the mice. Now, Dagon was the god of corn. It is thought that the plague was being spread by rats or mice. This particular plague, or kind of plague was being spread by this terrible scourge of rodents in the land. So, they had to make gold images of the mice or rats and gold images of the boils. This was the trespass offering.

Then, they also were told to make a new cart. They were to take two cows who have just given birth to calves, and take them away from their calves. They were to yoke these two together that have never been yoked before, never been harnessed before, onto this new cart and they had to put the ark on it. Then they were to let it go.

Now all of you know, I am quite sure that to ask such a ridiculous thing is almost to court disaster. Has anyone ever heard of bringing two cows that have never, ever before been harnessed? Not only that, but to take two who have just given birth to calves. Then, to put the two together and expect them, without any help whatsoever, to carry the cart back into the land they did not even know, where they had never been before. The whole thing was to be a miracle. The Philistines were told, that if these two hitherto unharnessed, unyoked cows can lead this cart back into a land by a way that they have never been before, even though they have taken them away from their own newly born calves, then this is the Lord. The story just simply but grandly says that when the two cows were harnessed, they went on the highway to Israel, lowing as they went.

When Israel saw the ark of the Lord coming back in that way, then I believe they knew the Lord was with them. You see, the Lord Himself can take care of His own work and His own testimony. He does not need us to go hurrying and scurrying around, trying to help Him, getting in the way. The Lord is well able. This was one of the greatest lessons for Samuel. He was living in days of tragedy, days of breakdown, days of failure. The easiest thing for Samuel would have been to go hurrying there, scurrying all over the place, trying to get the people together, trying to teach them, trying somehow to bring about a reformation. What would that have done? It would have been superficial; it would have been skin deep.

The first thing Samuel learnt was that God is sovereignly able to take care of His own testimony and of His own work. This was the first lesson he learnt. So, the ark came back into Israel without ever a battle having to be fought. It came back of its own accord. You know, I think of the story when it returned in chapter six. Some foolish men looked into it and died of the plague. Then at last, they brought it into its right place.

Then, we find in chapter seven verses 3–4 the beginning of the great reformation that was to last right the way through to the days of Solomon. Samuel calls the whole nation together at Mizpah. He says to them, "If you will only put away your gods, your idols, if you will only repent before the Lord, if you will only confess your condition, your sin to the Lord, then the Lord will once again own you and will deliver you." It says that all Israel gathered to Mizpah and it says, they confessed their sin before the Lord. They got down on their knees and they wept before the Lord, and it says they were as one man in coming before the Lord. They said, "This will we do."

Then Samuel offers up a sacrifice. As he does so, the Philistines begin to marshal their armies on the plain. Now, this is the interesting point. It was on that very plain, by that very stone Ebenezer, that Israel lost the battle and the ark was taken. Now, on that very plain, by that very rock, Israel was to be victorious. God always leads us back to the scene of failure. Where we failed is where we must be victorious. Where we succumbed is where we must overcome. We can never sort of circumvent things and come back there. We always have to come back to where we failed.

So, the rock was called Ebenezer, "Hitherto hath the Lord helped us" (verse 12). It was the beginning of a reformation. Samuel was not so foolish to think that it was the whole thing. He said, "Hitherto hath the Lord helped us." Now they march forward into a new phase altogether in God's dealings. The Philistines were completely routed and it says that in all the days of Samuel they never again bothered them.

Samuel's Circuit

Then you will notice in verse 15 of chapter ten, that Samuel had a circuit like the early Methodists. The circuit that he continually went round was Gilgal, Bethel, and Mizpah. His hometown, Ramah, was in the centre of a circle. He continually went round this circle to Bethel, to Gilgal, to Mizpah. (Shiloh was where the tabernacle was.) It is very interesting to find out the meanings of those places. You know, that which is connected with them: Bethel, the house of God, and all that that means. That was where he began his circuit. Each year his annual circuit began with the *house of God*.

From there he went on to Gilgal, which means *a wheel*. Do you know what it is connected with? It is connected with the putting up of the twelve stones of memorial on the banks of the river Jordan when the Lord said, "The reproach of Egypt I have wheeled off of you." It was the place where they were circumcised. It speaks of the cross circumcising our heart, our affections, our desires, our wills, our emotions, our minds, our intellects all coming under the circumcision of God. That is the cross. The house of God can be nothing, rendered futile, useless unless there is a knowledge of the cross which is circumcising all that we are naturally. Our natural man has got to come under the cross. It has got to come into the execution of God. It has got to come under the restriction and limitation of the Holy Spirit. That is the only way that the house of God can ever be built.

Mizpah means *watchtower*. It speaks of the need of eternal alertness and watchfulness if God is going to get value out of our being together and of our going on. Ramah, in the very heart of it all where he built an altar, it says means *high*. There, he lived.

You have there just a message in itself. In his annual circuit, as he moved around these things, note how often we find them. We find the *house of God*, and all that it means as the centre of God's work and of God's purpose, as the centre of all God's activity and of God's desire and satisfaction. Gilgal, the means by which God builds us together and fits us into our place and causes us to function, the circumcision of all that we are naturally. Cutting off all of it. Then there is Mizpah—watchtower. Oh, the need to watch, the need to watch and to pray, to watch unto prayer—that watchtower and Ramah, a heavenliness of character. That is Samuel's ministry and life.

Introduction to the Kingdom

Then, you find that the kingdom is introduced. Samuel brings in the kingdom. He introduces it. There is, of course, something very, very wonderful in the development of God's instrument. The way that the Lord slowly but surely develops the character of the man Samuel through those early days and then on into fuller maturity. There is a progressive development of character under the hand of the Spirit of God by the word of God.

Then we come to a point which really broke Samuel's heart. We find this, I am afraid to say, in many of the great men of God recorded for us in the Word. His heart's passion, it is quite obvious if he wrote this, certainly was to bring in God's king and to see the establishment of God's kingdom. Yet you see, oh, how cleverly the devil always seeks to somehow nullify God's activity. He will always do it by bringing in something counterfeit, something so like what God is after, such an imitation of what God is after. Outwardly, it seems right. Outwardly, it is perfect. Outwardly, there is absolutely no flaw. That is the way the devil always seeks to, somehow or other, thwart the Lord ever getting what He is really after by just building a counterfeit in its place, a substitute.

Often in the Christian life, this is so. It is as soon as we come to the Lord that the devil starts to try and get us off the ground upon which we came to the Lord. Then you get these multitudes and multitudes of Christians that have got a form of godliness. They are born again believers, but they only have a form of godliness. It is all self—self-made humility, self-made meekness, self-made patience, self-made forbearance, self-made love—it is all out of self. It is a kind of production of one's own personality and energy. Then, of course, as you all know, when the hammer of God falls on us, we do not know what is happening. We are knocked about all over the place and we think: "Oh, dear, what on earth happened to my Christian life? It has gone to pieces. It is all over the place." What is the Lord doing? He is smashing up something which is just ourselves, smashing up ourselves that He might bring in what is of God.

This is so, I am afraid, in so many companies of God's people. You get these New Testament setups, New Testament pattern places. They are just the means by which the devil takes hold of zealous, keen, out-and-out people and gets them absolutely sidetracked, because it is all the production of man, according to the word of God. Oh, we look into the word of God, we find how it is built, how it is ordered, and then we put it all together and it becomes the greatest stumbling to God's real thing. Thus the devil works, and this is how he does it: he gets a man like Saul, and he puts Saul in the way. That is what broke Samuel's heart. When the people came and said, "Make us a king," it was not that it was a shock to Samuel. He knew his whole life was a preparation for the king. Why was Samuel so grieved? Why did it break his heart? Why did he mourn? Why? It says, it was the little words, "Make us a king," that broke his heart. Then later on it is developed in the chapter, "We want a king like unto the other nations who will go out and come in before us, who will lead us into battle." What the people were saying was this: "We are not interested in God, who we cannot see. We want someone who will be our leader, who we can see, who will deliver us, upon whom we can depend, who will give us security and protection."

God's king will never be that. God's king himself will be a man so utterly dependent upon the Lord that when anything ever happened, he falls on his knees. But the people did not want that kind of king. They wanted a king who, when anything happened would brace himself up and say, "Come, all of you, go out to battle." A king that would get on his knees and say, "Now, Lord, what should we do? We have no strength. We have no might. We don't know what to do!" was not the kind of king the people wanted. They wanted someone like Achish, king of the Philistines, or someone like Agag, king of the Amalekites. They wanted someone who was tough and strong and hard and could lead the people.

That is what broke Samuel's heart. This was why the Lord said to Samuel, "Samuel," and this is a great lesson for us all, "give the people what they want." Now, this is one of the great principles of

God's dealing with us. If we ask long enough, we always get what we want. If the Lord refuses something to us, we can always know that we are in the way of God. When He does gives us everything we ask, it is a sign that something has got to be cured. The people asked for a king, and the Lord spoke to Samuel, "Samuel, listen to them; make them a king."

We find that Samuel has got to become part of something which was essentially counterfeit. That is why I have taken on this portion of Samuel to the 16th chapter where, of course, David is introduced. Well, Samuel is the instrument, at any rate, a very wonderful instrument indeed.

We can learn a tremendous amount from the whole attitude of Samuel in the way that he reacted: when a man's whole life is bound up with the bringing in of something and when at the very last point, it is thwarted and blasted. Then, in the end, in the grace of God, to have to put up with it all and see it all collapse and the tragedy of it. Then to just see a young man come forward who is the anointed of God. No wonder the Lord had to deal with Samuel.

Do you understand now why the Lord had to show Samuel that He was able to take care of His testimony and work? If Samuel had not learnt that lesson early in his life, he would never have been able to have persevered to the end. But he learnt his lesson and that is one of the most wonderful things about Samuel.

The Principles of Kingship

Then the next great section in this book is from chapter eight of I Samuel right through to chapter one of II Samuel. It is the comparison of these two men: Saul and David. We have called it the principles of kingship, as seen first negatively in Saul, and then positively in David. Now, I want you just to look at Saul and see some of the things about Saul. First of all, we do Saul a great injustice if we think that he was just an evil man. There were some very good qualities about Saul. I might point out that Saul in some ways was better than David. Now, let us look at some of those qualities. First, take chapter nine and verse two.

And he had a son, whose name was Saul, a young man and
a goodly: and there was not among the children of Israel
a goodlier person than he: from his shoulders and upward
he was higher than any of the people (1 Samuel 9:2).

Outwardly, then he was an outstanding man. He was an enormous man. He was a very tall man. He was head and shoulders above everyone else. That was one very good quality about him.

Then if we look at verse four, we find that he was also an industrious type of man. When his father said that the asses were lost, he did not just go around the Richmond locality. He evidently went as far up to Birmingham and over down to Salisbury looking for his father's asses. Quite a large area was covered in his concern for his father's asses. That was another very good quality, I might say, in these days when people are so careless.

Then in verse 21, we find that he was a very humble man. By the way, I might say that David was not necessarily a very humble man at the beginning. When Eliab said to David, "I know thy pride and the naughtiness of thy heart," he may have been speaking from experience. For when they anointed David, David did not flinch. David never fled and hid himself in the baggage. David never tried to get out of the way. David just stood there. Another thing about David was that when he went down to see Goliath, he had not the slightest concern or thought that he would not be able to take on Goliath. We know that it was faith, but there is a possibility that with David there was not quite the same so-called humility as we find in Saul. You find here Saul answered and said, "Am I not a Benjaminite, of the smallest of the tribes of Israel? And my family the least of all the families of the tribe of Benjamin? wherefore then speakest thou to me after this manner?"

Then in chapter ten and in verse 16, we find this:

And Saul said unto his uncle, He told us plainly that
the asses were found. But concerning the matter of the
kingdom, whereof Samuel spake, he told him not.

Then again, we shall find in verse 21 at the last part of that verse:

but when they sought him, he could not be found.

This was when they wanted to anoint him king. And in verse 22:

Therefore they asked of Jehovah further, Is there
yet a man to come hither? And Jehovah answered,
Behold, he hath hid himself among the baggage.

Those are some very good qualities about him. Then in chapter eleven and verse 13, it says:

And Saul said, There shall not a man be put to death this
day; for to-day Jehovah hath wrought deliverance in Israel.

That was over some men who refused to acknowledge him as
king. When a great victory was won, the people said, those men
that spoke evil of you, we will put to death. But Saul pleaded with
them for their safety and forgiveness, and he obtained it for them.
That is a very good quality.

Then you will find that Saul had many very good qualities
about him, but you will find that he was also very much in touch
with the things of God. If you look at 1 Samuel 10:1, we find:

then Samuel took the vial of oil, and poured
it upon his head, and kissed him

He was anointed. That speaks to us of being in touch with the
Holy Spirit. Then we read verse ten:

And when they came thither to the hill, behold, a
band of prophets met him; and the Spirit of God came
mightily upon him, and he prophesied among them.

So, he prophesied. That is also a very real connection with the
things of God. Then in verse 26, it says:

Saul also went to his house to Gibeah; and there went
with him the host, whose hearts God had touched.

Evidently, there was a relationship with others who felt the same about the things of God. And then chapter eleven and verse six:

And the Spirit of God came mightily upon Saul when he heard those words, and his anger was kindled greatly.

That was when he wrought the first great victory against the Philistines. Then in verse 15 of that same chapter:

and there they offered sacrifices of peace-offerings before the Lord; and there Saul and all the men of Israel rejoiced greatly.

In chapter 14 and verse 33, we find that Saul had a knowledge of the commandments of God contained in the book of Leviticus:

Then they told Saul, saying, Behold, the people sin against the Lord, in that they eat with the blood. And he said, Ye have dealt treacherously: roll a great stone unto me this day.

He found that after the battle, people were actually eating flesh with blood, which was, as you know, ruled out by the law of God. And he was very concerned about it. Verse 35:

And Saul built an altar unto the Lord: the same was the first altar that he built unto the Lord.

In verse 47 and 48, we find all his great victories recorded against the enemies of God.

Then in chapter 15 and verse 31, even when he finally and very terribly sinned against the Lord and was cut off from the kingdom, he worshipped the Lord. Now all this added up, means simply that there was a lot that was exceedingly good about Saul. I think probably today, if he was here, he would have been put in the front for testimony. He would have been leading teams. He would have probably been in the forefront of work for God because of his qualities. There was everything so much that was good about him. It was not only good, but evidently there was outwardly at any rate, a very real concern and exercise over the things of God.

Saul—the Natural Choice of the Natural Man

But we find that is just where things end. For Saul is a picture of the natural man, not of an evil, iniquitous natural man, but just simply of the natural man. All his good points, all his zeal, all his energy, all his natural understanding of the things of God, all that is wonderfully synthesised in Saul. Here he is, just the natural man. He has devoted all his good qualities to the Lord. He has devoted all his talents to the Lord. He is just completely, wholeheartedly in the service of God; but it is the natural man. That is why we find the two great instances of disobedience with Saul in chapter 13 and in chapter 15. In chapter 13:8–9, Samuel said to Saul, "Wait seven days and I will come and offer up the sacrifice." Now, this was just before they went out to do battle. It says expressly that Samuel did not come at the appointed time. Saul waited and waited and waited; and we must give him his credit; he waited a long time.

However, he began to see the people grow tired of waiting and they began to disperse. Many of the men began to go back to their homes saying, "Oh, we can't wait here any longer. We will have to go." He began to see all the army getting into disorder and discontent. He could not wait any longer. He said, "If I don't do something now, the people will all be dispersed." So, he took things into his own hands and offered up the sacrifice. As always, Samuel appeared the moment he had finished offering up the sacrifice. Do you remember what Samuel said? He said, "You have dealt presumptuously. The Lord has taken away the kingdom" (verses 13 and 14).

Then you find in chapter 15 that the word of the Lord came through Samuel to Saul to go out and destroy the Amalekites. When he went out to destroy the Amalekites, it says that he was told to destroy them utterly because of their sin. But we are told the Lord tells Samuel that he did not do it. When he comes back, he finds that Samuel says, "What is this bleating of sheep in my ear?" (verse 14). We remember the Lord clearly and decisively tells Saul that the kingdom has been taken away from him and given to another.

You see, the natural man has not got the capacity for going on in the things of God. The natural man has, as it were, much that can keep him to the point, but he does not have the capacity. When it really comes to real crises, he collapses. There is a veto upon the natural man in the things of God. You cannot find it more clearly than in the case of Saul. There was so much about him that was good. There was so much about him that was noble. There was so much about him that was commendable. There was much about him that was really what we would call zealous over the things of God. But, you see, he could not get through. There was a veto on it all. He collapsed.

David—the Shepherd Boy and Servant

You will find it very interesting that in many other ways, how different it is from David. For instance, notice the way that it is illustrated on the corporate side. David's army was literally pressed together to him. They were down and out. They were, many of them, brigands. They were men in debt, they were discontented, and they were forged together. But it is very different when you read the record of Saul, for it tells us that he chose these people. He went here and he went there, and he selected this one, he selected that one and others. It says, God touched their hearts, and they went with him. But, you know, you need a good deal more than to have your heart touched. That does not last very long. Some people have their hearts touched and they think, "Oh, I feel this is it. This is it. The Lord's here. I am with it." Out they come with you for a little while, until the storm hits them and some of the disillusionment and disappointment starts to break on them. They suddenly find out that it was not what they should be or not what they ought to be or not what they could be. Then, all the trouble begins. But you see, David's side, it was all very, very different. On David's side the men were pressed out. They had to go. They had to stay together. They were forced to keep together. There is such an amazing difference between the two.

We want to note something about Saul and that is this: the ease with which he comes to the throne. Although it expressly says that he did not want it, in many ways he came very easily to it. We do not find any long drawn out conflict over whether Saul should ever get to the throne or not. We find that he steps onto it very swiftly and easily and with great facility. It all happens very suddenly.

That is not so with David. David's is a long and drawn out story of the most terrible conflict to keep him from ever getting to the throne from the very beginning. You must see that at the very beginning. It is interesting to note with David that as a shepherd boy, God worked out a spiritual history. If it is true that some of the psalms that we have came from his earliest experiences as a shepherd lad, then that boy had a real experience of God, and he had a real experience of God's deliverances. That is the most remarkable thing. You do not often meet bears and lions. Yet as a lad, David met bears and lions and such like in the keeping of his father's sheep. He learnt some of the elementary principles of kingship.

For instance, he learnt that when you are given a flock to look after, you do not run when you see the lion coming. You take the lion by the beard, and you strangle him. This is the way David learnt some of his earliest lessons in kingship. That is why the Lord said, "I took thee from following after the sheep." Our Lord never allowed people to forget that it was the following after the sheep that had a connection with kingship in David's life.

You know, we make a great mistake if we think that when Goliath appeared on the scene, suddenly the Spirit of God came on David, and just like that he was able to go out and meet Goliath. Crises always find out what we are. If we have been indulgent, if we have been just letting things go on easily, if we have been taking things comfortably, a crisis will find us out. Suddenly, in the crisis, we shall sink, or we shall shine.

David was the only one that had something behind him which qualified him to meet that. The way that he spoke, the way that he went out, the way that Saul drooped his armour all over him and said, "Now then, come on, you can't go out without armour on you." But evidently David was quite small, although he was well formed. Evidently, he was not a tall fellow like Saul and Saul's armour must have just literally drooped off him. David said to Saul, "I have not proved it. Just you allow me to have the things that I have proven." That is one of the principles of kingship. Kingship means you are not afraid of saying where you stand and what measure you have attained to. Paul could say, "I am what I am by the grace of God."

There is such a lot of this stupid kind of idea amongst the people of God that you must not let on. You must not say, "I don't know," or, "I haven't experienced that." Above all, you must not say, "I've not seen that." Always you must have seen. Always you must know. That is one of the things that never comes to the throne. You will find that the greatest saints and the people who have gone on the farthest are people who can say, "I have not seen that point, that is something the Lord has not yet shown me. I don't quite understand." Great saints can learn from a child.

It is one of the principles of kingship. David learnt it. It was no good him going out in armour that he had never proved and never worn and did not know anything about. All he wanted was his shepherd garments. All he wanted was his five stones which he had selected himself and his sling. Those were things he knew all about. Those were things he had proved. Those belonged to himself in his own history and with that, he could go out in the name of God.

If David had gone out in Saul's armour, there would have been a tragedy. David could only go out in what was his own history and experience. In that, he could trust the Lord and there was victory. That must always be the way we come to the throne. Each step must be real. Each step must be genuine. Each step must be true, inward history. That was how David came to the throne.

Then you find that he is in Saul's household and it says that Saul watched him day and night to see if he could kill him. It is not very easy to live under the same roof with someone who watches you like that—listens to your words, watches your actions, watches your gestures, watches the facial expression, just watches every single movement. Three times this little word is found in that chapter: "And David behaved himself wisely before the king." There again is a principle of kingship: circumspection. How to walk circumspectly. How to abstain from all appearance of evil. How to be able to live in an atmosphere poisoned by hate and criticism and malice and jealousy. How to live in it and to be able, in the end, to walk through it without giving any ground at all. That is another principle of kingship.

What did Saul know about these principles? He knew nothing. He came to the throne overnight. David's was to be a long, drawn out history of learning in a very hard school those things which could qualify him for the throne.

May the Lord teach us some things. Here we are in a day in which surely the kingdom of God is in its more outward way and the King has to be brought back.

We have much to learn from Hannah and much to learn from Samuel in the way that the king is brought back. There is so much today, individually and corporately, which is like Saul.

Outwardly, it is fine. Outwardly, it is head and shoulders above the rest. Outwardly, it has got many good qualities. Outwardly, it, as it were, can carry things. But when put to the test, it is disobedient to the heavenly vision. It cannot go through to the end. When it is put to the acid test, murderous jealousy is discovered and exposes any kind of readiness to take advantage trying to get there by the quickest shortcut. All that is Saul, and today we have it. Now, that is not God's way, and it is not God's thought. God has to work in a hidden, inward way to bring His people through a long and drawn out school of real discipline and suffering and education that He might bring them, in the end, into kingship.

3.
Contrasting
Saul and David

We will start where we left off at 1 Samuel 16. We are on the second main section of these two books, which is the principles of kingship as revealed in Saul and David. We have already dealt with the first section, which was "The instrument to introduce the king and the kingdom." Now we are upon that section from 1 Samuel 8 to 11 Samuel 1, which is what we have called in our outline "principles of kingship" as revealed negatively in Saul and positively in David.

Remember, we have considered Saul. We looked at his good qualities. We noticed his relationship to the things of God. We noticed his disobedience. We noticed what he conceived to be the corporate nature of things. We also saw how he ended. Writing, as it were, an epitaph over him, we noticed how easily he came to the throne. There was an absence of conflict, of antagonism, and of opposition. Everything, generally speaking, except for one or two very small, almost insignificant exceptions, was for Saul to come to the throne and contributed to bringing him to the throne.

Now we come to David, and of course, the record is largely taken up with David. Saul really is only given a certain number of chapters and even then, is only, as it were, preparing the way for God's man by contrast. The books of Samuel are mostly taken up with this man, David.

A Hidden Preparation

The first thing we want to note in the principles of kingship is to look at David as the shepherd lad. We find this in chapters 16 and 17. (I wish we could take the Psalms that were written by David and find out how they give to us a key to his life in these different periods, but that is another study altogether.) We see him in these two chapters as the shepherd boy or the shepherd lad. We have a tremendous amount to learn about David from this question of his very early history and experience of God.

Now, you know, in these studies we have not sought to avoid some of the technical difficulties because we have felt that it was good to look at them. The books of Samuel are probably some of the most difficult in the Bible for discrepancies. We have to admit that there are discrepancies in these two books of Samuel. We have to say that in truthfulness and honesty before God, yet without in any way impairing our faith or confidence in this as the word of God, it is utterly and completely inspired. We cannot take too much time with the discrepancies, but there are quite a few. They are largely to do, of course, with the way that these two books of Samuel do not always corroborate with the two books of Chronicles. Sometimes we find different figures given to the same time. Hebrew is a language, particularly on the numerical side, given to a very real possibility of mistakes being made by copyists, particularly in actual numbers.

If you have read these books with your wits about you, one of the discrepancies you will have noticed is that chapters 16 and 17 seem to contradict one another. First of all, we find in chapter 16, from verse 14 to verse 23, that David is brought in to Saul as a skilful musician and Saul so loved him that he made him his armour bearer. Evidently, every time that this mental sickness came upon Saul, David was brought in and played for him. An armour bearer is not just some small thing, but is one of the most honoured, if not *the* most honoured position that a man could hold in the personal company of people who are around the king.

Compare those verses to 1 Samuel 17:55–58.

And when Saul saw David go forth against the Philistine, he said unto Abner, the captain of the host, Abner, whose son is this youth? And Abner said, As thy soul liveth, O king, I cannot tell. And the king said, Inquire thou whose son the stripling is. And as David returned from the slaughter of the Philistine, Abner took him, and brought him before Saul with the head of the Philistine in his hand. And Saul said to him, Whose son art thou, thou young man? And David answered, I am the son of thy servant Jesse the Beth-lehemite (1 Samuel 17:55–58).

In the first few verses of chapter 18, we find again that David had been taken into the household and service of Saul. It would seem that there is some discrepancy, but the key to it all is twofold. First, these scriptures are not giving us a chronology.

They are giving us a history which at every point is utterly correct, but a history which is so constituted, so patterned, so ordered, that it is bringing out a spiritual history. I am quite sure some of the reasons why we find all this in chapter 16 (which some believe belongs to a slightly later time after he had slain Goliath) are because the Lord is wanting to show that David had a hidden history. This is preparation for kingship or dominion. No man has ever been brought to the throne of God who does not have such a history.

Listen to this that is found in chapter 16, starting in verse 18:

Then answered one of the young men, and said, Behold, I have seen a son of Jesse the Beth-lehemite, that is skilful in playing, and a mighty man of valor, and a man of war, and prudent in speech, and a comely person; and Jehovah is with him.

This reveals to us a hidden history. For instance, we know for a fact that all these things are qualities that are going to be tempered and tried so as by fire in these next years of David's life. He is introduced to us on the scene immediately with these qualities.

One of the qualities we find, for instance, is that he is skilful in playing the harp. This means that David practised. It was not just an intuitive gift. It was not just simply that it was something born in him—no doubt it was, it was part of David—but it was something which needed careful practice. A man who can kill a lion and can kill a bear has got to keep his touch on the heart. This is just one aspect in the hidden history of David's life.

He was a man of valour. Now, why should we have, not only a man of valour, but also a man of war? Not all men of war are men of valour. This has been proved again and again. We find that there are men of war. They are in the business of war. They are in the business of fighting, and yet they are not mighty men of valour. In all Saul's army, there was only one man who we could say has got that quality of courage which was drawn out of him in the moment of fiery trial. Yet all these are mighty men, Abner included. Here you find David had something about him uniquely proven, and it was something developed by God when David was watching sheep.

He was a man of war, a very mature man of war. When you have experienced things, whilst you are firm, you are also full of grace. There is something prudent about your speech, something wise about your speech, something careful about your speech, not hypocritical tactfulness. A lot of tact, of course, is just hypocrisy, but prudence in speech is a gift of the Holy Spirit.

Then, he was a comely person. The Septuagint puts it more in our own language, "a handsome person." There was something about David that was handsome. Of course, he was marked out. His other brothers were evidently outstanding men. David was slightly shorter than the others. Of course, he was younger, but he had auburn hair and he had very pale eyes, if we take the description of him: "he was fair of eyes," or "very beautiful of eye." Both these things marked him out as a person that was uniquely beautiful to look at. There was something comely about David. I believe, of course, that because of that, it is quite obvious that David took care of himself. He was not just a ruin or wreck of a person to even look at. There was something about him which must have impressed you. It says simply and sums it all up: "the Lord was with him."

Here then, at the very beginning of the introduction of God's man for the throne, are these qualities that all come out of a hidden history. We know very little about the hidden history of David, yet we believe the 23rd Psalm certainly comes from the very early part of his life, possibly written even at the time of which we are now speaking. Here was someone who had not only a very real experience in these ways, which showed these qualities, but had above all, through it all, an experience of God.

This is what is revealed in his experience with Goliath. If you will read with me just a few verses, I think the Word itself will speak to us much more than I can. 1 Samuel 17:26:

> *And David spake to the men that stood by him, saying, What shall be done to the man that killeth this Philistine, and taketh away the reproach from Israel? for who is this uncircumcised Philistine, that he should defy the armies of the living God?*

As we have already said, this is a lad of about 16 who was speaking. He already knows what it is to have a reproach upon his nation. Even though he is young, he feels keenly the fact that the people of God have been dishonoured. There is something soiled about the people of God, and he reveals to us that it is not just patriotism. He shows to us quite clearly by his words that it is the living God's name that is the root of his concern. This is something that has come out of an experience which is largely hidden. We do not know about it. We do not know what he learned looking after the sheep, but we do know that it came out in his experience with Goliath.

If you look at verse 37, you find here again another key to David's spiritual condition and character.

And David said, the Lord that delivered me out of
the paw of the lion, and out of the paw of the bear, he
will deliver me out of the hand of this Philistine.

Faith does not just suddenly fall on us. When we are found in a situation, faith is the product of a history. When we have a routine history with the Lord, then, when we are in a crisis, that history is proved. Faith does not suddenly come out to keep us at the right moment. We must remember. Here, there was something that came out of a history.

Then, in verses 45–47, we find something else:

Then said David to the Philistine, Thou comest to me with
a sword, and with a spear, and with a javelin: but I come to
thee in the name of the Lord of hosts, the God of the armies of
Israel, whom thou hast defied. This day will the Lord deliver
thee into my hand; and I will smite thee, and take thy head
from off thee; and I will give the dead bodies of the host of
the Philistines this day unto the birds of the heavens, and
to the wild beasts of the earth; that all the earth may know
that there is a God in Israel, and that all this assembly may
know that the Lord saveth not with sword and spear: for the
battle is the Lord's, and he will give you into our hand.

That does surely reveal a history—hidden from our gaze, but a history. Here is a boy of 16, speaking words that we ourselves would find difficult to say. He gets right to the root of the whole matter. Not only before the unbelievers, but before the Lord's people, who are in such a state of disorder, fear, timidity, and despair, he is able to say words like this—one lad against a host, and without even the backing of his own kith and kin. He had already been rebuked by his brother for the naughtiness of his heart and for his pride, yet he is able to talk like this. That, I say, shows to us that there is a history behind David which was beaten out in his looking after sheep.

David's Character Being Built

Through His Bitter Experiences

Then, in chapter 18, you will find David in the household of Saul. You know that one of the most difficult things of all, and a thing which many people crack up under, is to live under the same roof with someone who is violently antagonistic. Kingship comes out of this kind of atmosphere. It comes out, not only of the way that we develop the gifts of God in us, and the way that we diligently fulfil the functions that God has given us. It comes out not only over the truly inwrought experience that we gain in our routine, everyday business life. But it comes out of situations of jealousy, of hatred, of suspicion, and of poisonous insinuation. When people have got to live under the same roof and in the atmosphere of murderous malice, this is where kingship comes out. There is nothing like this atmosphere to destroy us spiritually. Many people cannot put up with that. They can put up with anything else, but they cannot put up with living under a roof with anything like that—with whisperings, with talk, with gossip, with suspicion, and insinuation. How that takes hold of our old natures, and how it kills them. It cannot kill the new nature, but it can destroy the old. We hate to be slummed. We hate to be thought of as in the wrong. We hate to be maligned. We hate to have people engineering things against us. We hate it when people we know are talking and banding themselves together in corners. That is the thing that will draw out any self-interest in us and bring it right out into the open.

It says three times in the record that David behaved wisely, and he learnt through that bitter experience. It is a very rare and unusual thing to find someone behaving wisely in such an atmosphere. It is just in that situation that we behave very unwisely. We either answer back or we start to come down to the same level of engineering things, or whispering, or answering or arguing, or all the rest of it. We come down to that level so quickly. But to behave wisely is a gift of God. It is something which only the Lord can do in us when our hearts are wholly towards Him. That is one of the principles of kingship: a spirit that is prepared to live ungrieved in the presence of every kind of malice.

Through His Time as a Fugitive

If you go on, you will find David as the fugitive. From verse 19 right the way on to II Samuel 1, we find David as the fugitive. This is a very necessary part of God's school for kingship. He hounds us. He allows us to be in a wilderness. He allows us to know what storms are. He allows us to know what barrenness is. He allows us to know all the things that can afflict us, all the things that can pile up in front of us as evidence that the Lord has forsaken us. You know, the rabbis said, and Josephus records that when Samuel anointed David, as he bent over to anoint him, he whispered in his ear that he was the chosen one of God for the throne. Whatever it is, it is quite obvious that David did know in his heart that the Lord had His hand on him for the throne. Yet, you can imagine how in this wilderness period of his life, he must have questioned time and time again as to whether it was not all a very fanciful delusion. I think we shall find out that once or twice he thought it was.

At Naioth

The first place we find him as a fugitive is in Naioth, where Samuel lived (see 1 Samuel 19:18–24). What has that to teach us about kingship? It teaches us the value of instruction, for David found himself amongst the prophets. There, he totally poured out his heart to Samuel. There, he told him all that had happened and no doubt Samuel took the word of God and instructed him. It says that they dwelt together in Naioth of Ramah. You see, that is one of the things we have to learn: that we need instruction. We have to be prepared to be instructed by those older than ourselves. We have got to learn from those who possibly belong to another phase. There is a very foolish school abroad which thinks that you must not be educated, you must not be instructed in any way unless it is through someone in your own phase, but this is not so. We must be those who can take a man like Samuel. Samuel was not the king. Samuel was not actually in the kingdom as such. He belonged to the phase that ended the judges and introduced the kingdom. Yet David, as God's chosen king, could put himself into the hands of Samuel for instruction. You know, the Lord has a wonderful way, when we put ourselves into the hands of others, of undoing all the attempts of the enemy to undo us.

Saul sent a band of armed men to Samuel and David at Naioth. Then he sent another band, then he sent a third band. What happened to each successive band as they came to the prophets? They, themselves, prophesied and that was the end; they joined the prophets. In the end, Saul comes to find out. He has decided that he himself will murder David. He will put an end to David. But when Saul comes, before Saul even gets near the prophets, he starts to prophesy. That is the reason that we have the little proverb, "Is Saul also among the prophets?" This is the way the Lord can undo things when we are wholly given into His hands.

That is the first thing we learn about David the fugitive. In spite of the fact that he knew something of God's purpose, he was prepared to learn from others. He was prepared to just simply be with others. If God has given you any gift, any function, you will lose nothing by putting yourself unreservedly and in a way that is completely submissive into the hands of others. You will not lose anything. If God has something for you, He will bring it all out. He will draw it out, He will develop it, He will show it to everyone else, and He will bring it out into the clear in the end. Every attempt to finish you off, to eliminate you, will be met by the Lord Himself in a very wonderful way.

At the Stone of Ezel

The next thing we find is in chapter 20. There we find the rather wonderful but sad story of the stone of Ezel and Jonathan.

You remember Saul tried to murder David. Three times he tried to murder him. He got away from him twice. Then he went back into the household of Saul, and again he tried to do it. In the end, David comes to Jonathan and begs him to do something. Jonathan says he will find out, and they agree on a little plan. Jonathan tells David, "You stay here and hide, and I'll come out and I'll shoot arrows as if I'm just practising. If I tell the lad to come back and bring the arrows, you know you can stay. You can come out and come back with me. Saul will have you in his home again. But if I shoot the arrows beyond the lad and tell him to go on quickly, then you will know that Saul determines to murder you. You must get out as quickly as you can."

Well, you know the story. It is there for you to read. But what does it teach us? The word *Ezel* means "demarcation" or "separation." This stone is called the stone of separation and truly it was. Here were two people who loved each other. They truly loved each other. But it was the kind of relationship that would not go through to the throne. It was a relationship that in the end, ended—Jonathan to stay with Saul, although he knew that David was to be king, and David to depart from Jonathan, only to see him once more in his life. It is very beautiful the way that Jonathan says to David, "The Lord be between thee and me." In other words, the Lord be the union, the Lord be our oneness. Between me and you, the Lord is our oneness. He is the common thing about us both. But you see, in spite of all Jonathan's protestation, in spite of Jonathan's very real and genuine love and concern for David, Jonathan ends in death, slain by the Philistines. He never comes to the throne.

In the very next few chapters, the very next few verses, we find Adullam. There at Adullam are 400 men, but their love for David was not pure like Jonathan's. Their relationship to David was not like Jonathan's. Yet those 400 came to the throne, and Jonathan was rejected and died on the battlefield at the hand of the Philistines. What does this teach us? It just simply teaches us that the purest friendship, the most beautiful friendship, the most real love, unless it is prepared to so identify itself with that which it loves, then it can lose everything: position, father, mother, home, all thought of coming to the throne. Unless it is prepared for that, it will not end up in the throne. It will end up in death at the hands of the enemy. A terrible thought. Yet the stone of Ezel is the stone of separation. Only once more in Jonathan's life, and that for a brief few moments in a forest, was he to hold communion with David.

Let us learn from that lesson. There are many such associations in the Christian world today. There are people, and congregations of people, with very beautiful love for one another. It is something very touching, very pure, very genuine, but it is not going to end in the throne. It is something that must die at the hands of the enemy. When put to the most acid test of all, it does not get to the throne. Let us learn then, from that period of David's life.

At the Tabernacle at Nob

The next period is in the first part of chapter 21. Here we find that David is at the tabernacle at Nob. There in the tabernacle he inquires of God. We see two or three things: he inquires of God in the house of God, he is fed in the house of God, and he receives the very sword with which he slew Goliath. What does this teach us? It teaches us one simple thing: that within the house of God, our past victories are there for the present. Isn't that a wonderful thing? Things which belong to our past history are kept in the house of God for present need. Elsewhere, we lose them. The house of God is the greatest preserving factor in the universe. There our life is preserved. There our contribution is preserved. There our fruit abides. There our victories are kept.

That is a lesson we have to learn. We find that alone we can fall, but in the house of God we are preserved. David learnt a very deep, hard lesson in the tabernacle. But he is given the bread which is going to keep him alive, and he is given the sword with which to fight, out of the house of the Lord. Albeit there is much weakness about his manner and attitude in the house of God.

At Gath of the Philistines

Next we find that we have a very sad little interlude in David's life as a fugitive. He evidently feels that perhaps the whole thing is a fanciful dream. He wonders at all this set against him, he, one man. With everything ranged against him, he flees into Gath of the Philistines. There, he thinks he will be safe, only to his horror to find out that there he is less safe than ever. Then David has to get out of Gath of the Philistines by scrabbling on the doors and feigning madness.

You know, that is just what happens with some of us when we are in this battle for the throne and the house of God. There are times when we think it is all a fanciful dream and there is far, far too much against us. Here we are alone—a little insignificant group, absolutely alone. Perhaps we feel almost like an individual left alone. Very few people understand, very few people are going to commit themselves to such a way. Oh, they will rest on things that have already been gained in past church history, but anything new to be revealed, anything new to come out, anything new to be recovered, and you will find it cut right down to the tiniest little handful. There will be times when you just really wonder whether, quite honestly, it is all a fanciful dream. "Why hasn't everyone else seen? Why aren't they all coming flocking forward? Why do we get left like this?"

Sometimes we get off the ground the Lord gave and we go onto natural ground. We get into situations that are foolish, and the only way out is by sheer humiliation, by just having to get ourselves out of the scrape we have got ourselves into. There is a lesson to be learned there about getting off God's ground onto natural things.

At the Cave of Adullam

Then, we also find in chapter 24 that David comes out of Gath of the Philistines with a great lesson learned, and he goes up into a cave. Now, this is very interesting, because evidently, he comes out of Gath of the Philistines alone, and goes into the cave of Adullam alone. As far as he is concerned, he is the only one, but he is perfectly sure that the Lord is going to fulfil His purpose in one way or another. God has got the first foundational thing laid in David's life. He has got one man now prepared to go through. From that He begins to expand, and we find that 400 come. I cannot say that these men are exactly beautiful in character or in their relationship. We would call them brigands. We would call them outlaws. They were men who were in debt. They were men who were discontented with things. They were people who were bitter of soul—400 of them. No doubt, if we could see them today, we would just wonder quite who and what they were. But here they are, contrasted with the very beautiful friendship of Jonathan. These 400 mighty men of David are to come to the throne and are to hold all kinds of positions in the kingdom of God. That is something for us to learn.

In that cave (and that name of *Adullam* means "resting place"), in that cave was beaten out a very real experience of a life together. I do not suppose for a moment, if we could question the 400, they would have called it a resting place. But it was called a resting place because it was God's resting place, not their resting place as such. A lot was being dealt with there in that cave, but it was God's resting place, the place where God was progressively getting His rest. He was forging an instrument there in that cave, which was to produce a kingdom.

Modern exploration has revealed to us a lot of things. One of them is that if this cave of Adullam still exists, it could only possibly accommodate 250 at the very most. I think this is rather interesting to think that of all the caves in the Bethlehem and Adullam area they feel none of them could have accommodated the number that are here mentioned without very real difficulties. They would have been living on top of each other. There are books which go into the reason why some of the larger caves in the area are definitely ruled out as being the location of the cave of Adullam. But those caves that could be, could only accommodate a smaller number. That speaks volumes as to the very real difficulties there must have been for those men as they had to get through the situation together.

Then we find in chapter 23 that David has to learn another very deep lesson, and that is the treachery and the shallowness of the people of God in many ways. You find him here in one case being hunted into the wilderness. They are only too prepared, just for diplomatic and political reasons, to give up David to Saul. They will mark him and give him away. In another place, he delivers a whole city from the Philistines. Yet, he is told by the Lord that when Saul comes against them, they will deliver him up without even a conscience about it.

He learns deeply and bitterly what is in humanity, and this is one of the principles of kingship. We learn what is in one another. We do. We learn what is in one another. We find out the capacity for treachery; just that capacity for shallowness, for political engineering, for diplomatic movements. Oh, how quickly the Lord's people will sacrifice one another at times just for diplomacy, just for sheer politics. Some people will greet you, and smile at you, and will shake your hand at certain occasions, but will cut you dead at others. They do not want to see you or have anything to do with you sometimes, because it just does not serve their purpose. At other times, they will be all over you and all around you, very sweet and nice. You have to learn that, if you are going to come to the throne in any way.

Another thing you also have to learn is the exact opposite in yourself. In chapters 24 to 26, you find three things that David has to learn. Twice Saul is brought into his hand, and twice his men say, "Come on, let's kill him. The Lord has delivered Saul into your hand. The kingdom is actually yours. He is there for you to take." But each time, David deliberately allows Saul to escape. He will not move as much as a finger to bring the kingdom nearer to himself, to bring the throne nearer. The other, of course, is the story of Abigail and Nabal, whose name means "fool." He was a very prosperous man, a very successful man, a self-made man, but a very foolish man. He was a man who was very, very short with David's young men that were sent down to receive provision and payment for the protection that they had given to Nabal's shepherds. Do you know what happens? David is so angry that he decides he will wipe out Nabal and his whole family and everything to do with it; he is furious with the whole situation. But Abigail, a woman of tremendous capability and wisdom, saddles an ass and collects together a whole amount of provision and goes out to meet him on the way and turns away his thought. She says two interesting things. First, she says, "You don't want to be guilty of the shedding of blood." Secondly, she says, "You don't want to avenge yourself."

This was the deep lesson that David had to learn. To never take anyone's life needlessly and, secondly, not to avenge himself. Not to destroy someone to bring the kingdom nearer, to gain an advantage. Secondly, not ever to seek to vindicate himself. Now, this is one of the deepest principles of kingship in actual fact. It is one which, in a sense, embodies everything else. The sheer refusal to take or make any advantages to bring yourself nearer the throne or the fulfilment of God's purpose concerning it, and the refusal in any way whatsoever to vindicate oneself or avenge oneself even when the opportunity is given.

Do you know that the Lord will give us opportunities? He will deliberately give us opportunities of vindicating ourselves, of avenging ourselves upon those that have done us wrong, just in order to bring us to the place where either something in us is exposed or we learn the deepest lesson that is the very foundation of the throne. The Lord Jesus Himself, the Lamb upon the throne, personifies all this by refusing completely, in any way at all, to make or take advantage or to vindicate Himself, right through to the end. That is the very principle of the throne of God. So, we learn some very deep lessons.

With the King of the Philistines

But then we come to the last part of this book, and we find that it is all bound up with the Philistines again. It is amazing that after David has learnt such a deep lesson, he suddenly is taken by fear and flees into the Philistine country. He takes all 600 of his men with him, and they actually become part of King Achish's bodyguard. It is an amazing situation for someone who is marked out for the throne of God to become so compromised that they are actually bolstering up the enemies of God.

Now, this is exactly what can happen to you and to me. It is not something fanciful, it is not a dream, it is not imaginative. We may be being brought by the grace of God to dominion, to the throne, but just because we are being brought by God to such a place, the enemy will come in on every avenue he can. Do you know that we can actually be found supporting the enemies of God? We can be engineered into such a situation by circumstances that we are in fact bolstering up the very forces that are against the people of God and the interests of God.

David is given a city of the Philistines—that is putting God in debt for a start. I do not know whether you have ever had an experience like that where the enemy makes you a gift and puts you in a debt to himself. He gives you a place, a nicely feathered nest, something that is very pleasant and opportune and helpful, but he is putting you into his debt. When the Philistines go out to war with the people of God, David has got to come out with them. He is actually found in the very armies that are marching against the interest, and the purpose, and the people of God. He is put in *the* place of confidence by the enemy of God. He is put in the rear with the king himself.

David learns bitterly his lesson. When there is division in the ranks of the enemy and they say, "We are not going to have that man bringing up the rear. He might well play the traitor to the lot of us. Send him back!" Look at this man, this great man of God. Now he is brought in and he is tipped out at the will of little minions, the people whose champion he met and destroyed. Now he is being ordered about here and there as they wish. When he goes back to Ziklag, he finds everything is lost and his own choice 600 speak of stoning him.

David has come to rock bottom. He has lost his home, his wives, and the others have lost everything. But you know the story: how they took the 600 quickly and pursued after the Amalekites; how 200 of them got faint on the way and stopped by the brook Besor. The 400 went on and caught them and found everyone safe. They destroyed the Amalekites, except for some young men that got away on camels. They brought back all the wives, the children, and the spoil. Then David was not finished. For the 400 then said, we will not share the spoil with the 200 who were faint. David has to settle a principle that those that stand by the baggage and those that fight at the front must all share the spoil. It became a statute in Israel forever.

Well, that is the end of David as a fugitive. He comes to the throne. Saul dies in that very battle with the Philistines in which David was involved, but by the grace of God, David was removed in the nick of time. We find that to come to the throne of God there is conflict, there is privation, there is every kind of affliction. There is satanic antagonism. There must be a bitter experience of human life in every form. There is no such thing as these dear old ladies that fill up Christian circles, who have no idea of what this life is about and no experience of it. They are so separated in a wrong way, that they do not even know how the world thinks. They can only gather their skirts around and flee at the very smell of tobacco—a terrible thing. That is not an experience of life—treachery, shallowness, superficiality, its sorrows and its joys. The stuff that goes behind Psalms is a history of human experience in fullness in every way. It is also an experience of God, a deep, hidden experience of the Lord. That is what brings a man and a woman to the throne. Let us learn, then, from David, as God's man, how wonderfully that is exemplified.

A Kingdom Established

Hebron

Lastly, we find the rest of the chapters are taken up from II Samuel 2 to chapter 20 with the establishment of the kingdom. It is the throne established. This is seen in three distinct phases. Firstly, we find David at Hebron in chapters 2–5. Now, what does Hebron mean?

God has brought his man to the throne. David is crowned king of Judah. For seven and a half years, he reigns over just the tribe of

Judah, but we find now that everything has got to be consolidated. All the principles that we have seen expressed and displayed have now got to be established and consolidated.

Where does the Lord teach at first? What is the first thing the Lord does? He brings them to a place called Hebron. What does Hebron mean? It has the most interesting meaning. First it means a *ford* and from then, we are told, because it was a ford it came to mean a *company*. How can a company and a ford be associated together? Simply like this: there is a ford over a river and any number of people coming to cross that river are narrowed down to one point on the river over which they must go. So the word Hebron came to mean not only a ford, but a company of people going the same way. So, it came to mean fellowship. We understand it as fellowship. What does it mean? It means many people narrowed down to one ford. They have all got to go over the same course. This is how God consolidates His kingdom. Once He has, as it were, brought us into the kingdom, He has to consolidate everything. He does it this way: we are crowned at Hebron. What does that mean? It means that by association, in union with other children of God, we come to the throne. There is no other way. No individuals will sit on thrones, as many people so foolishly think. There is nowhere that you will find it in the Scriptures. There are not millions of crowns each to be apportioned out to millions of saints upon millions of thrones. You will not find that. You will find one throne and a bride with one crown. It is a bride that is crowned as the queen of God's king. One throne with a king and a queen.

That means that to come to the throne, we have to be associated together. We have to be bound together, fused together, welded together, knit together. That is why David was crowned at Hebron, nowhere else—Hebron. It was there that he was crowned. There, he was crowned king of Israel; not only king of Hebron, but seven and a half years later, king of Israel.

The Consolidation of the Kingdom

We won't stay more with that. You must read it yourself. You will find some very interesting things there in those chapters from two to five. First of all, we find Abner and Joab. This man, Joab—what an interesting character study this man Joab is. He has been used of God to consolidate the kingdom and yet, oh, what a terrible trial he was to David! What a hard man Joab was, and yet God sometimes needs hard men. Sometimes He has to associate a very hard man with a very soft man. David, in his heart, was a very gentle man. Joab, in his heart, was a very severe man. Oh, what Joab did when he took that city of Ammon, how he sawed the people, how he put them under those threshing instruments of iron, how he made them pass through the brick kilns to destroy them. What a hard man.

When Abner came to try and make a pact and covenant with David, and indeed succeeded in doing so, do you know what Joab did? He followed Abner out, took him into the gate, and slew him. When, later on, another nephew of David's came to a high position under Absalom and was later appointed by David to a position of trust, Joab slew him as he kissed him. Yet this man and the way he ended, was used of God.

David learnt from bitter experiences in the consolidation of the kingdom through that man Joab. You find again and again he says, "Oh, you sons of Zeruiah," that was his sister. "You sons of Zeruiah. You are too hard." They did many things. We learn from this that our friends often give us more grief and trial than ever our enemies. David spent many a sleepless night, I am sure, over Joab, more than he did over others.

Zion

Then we find from chapter five and the few chapters to chapter 10, just a few interesting things. They are tremendous things, really, because for the first time, the heart of it all is opened for us. We find suddenly that Zion is captured. This is the first real point in Scripture when the city of God comes into view. It has been wonderful through our studies up to now just to see how, at each point through the different books, different things have come in for the first time in the word of God. Here, for the first time, Jerusalem comes on the scene. Up to now it is "Jebu-salem," the royal city of the Jebusite. Now it is Zion, the Zion of God, the perfection of beauty, God's holy habitation. Everything is to be summed up in Zion—Jerusalem, the city of God. There the temple is going to be.

Now, mark the wonderful way in which God is working. First, we must capture Zion. So, David goes up to Zion and of course, Zion was a stronghold, and they said, "Oh, dear, dear, dear. The lame and the blind can stop David from taking Jebu-salem." But David and Joab, found a wonderful means of getting into Jebu-salem, especially as we know today. They found a shaft that had been cut by the Jebusites for water and up along that shaft they poured into the city and took it. So Jebu-salem became Jerusalem. It became the city of God and David's capital—a place for the temple and the house of God. That is a very wonderful thing to find, first of all, that here is something taken for God. God gets the ground, now mark that. He gets the ground first.

The Ark

The second thing we find is the ark. The ark is the symbol of the presence of God. When God has the ground, the presence of God comes. It is very interesting, for instance, at Pentecost. When the Lord gathered together 120 in an upper room, in a certain geographical locality, the presence of God came. First you get the ground; then the presence of God comes. The presence of God commits Himself to saints on God's ground. Then you will have the house of God.

The House of God

There are three things in these chapters. First, Zion: that is the ground. Secondly, the ark of God: that is the presence of God committed to His people on that ground. Thirdly, the house of God. David opens his heart up before the Lord to tell Him what he really wants to do. He wants to build a house for the Lord. The Lord tells him to postpone all that. He replies that He will build David a house.

We learned some very wonderful lessons about the ark as it is taken up. It was taken up, you know, on an ox cart; a new ox cart. They followed the Philistine device, and it was a mistake. Then when it came to a rut in the road and the ark nearly slipped off, Uzzah put forth his hand and died for his presumption. This again is just one more piece of evidence of this simple principle running through it all: God takes care of His own work. This is the basic thing about kingship. You cannot vindicate yourself. You cannot make or take advantages. You cannot, as it were, further your own cause or position in this question of kingship. It has got to be the Lord, utterly.

David learned a very big lesson. He learned that he had not read the Scripture. He should have known that it was the Levites who bore the ark upon their shoulders. So, he leaves it in the house of Obed-Edom, who was a Kohathite and they are the very section of the Levites that were meant always to carry the furniture of the most holy place on their shoulders. That is why the Lord blesses the house of Obed-Edom. Later, it is brought up into Jerusalem by the Levites and the Lord is with them. There was great rejoicing.

So, we find there in those few chapters something, I think, that reveals the heart of it all. It is the consolidation of the kingdom. But what is the kingdom for? The kingdom is not something in itself. The kingdom is for the habitation of God. So, here you have it. First Zion, then the ark of God, and now the first talk of the building of the house of the Lord. Isn't that wonderful? First the Lord commits Himself to His people when they are on the right ground, and then He starts the building of the house.

But I want you to notice that there are a lot of victories recorded from chapters 8–10. What do we find about these victories? We find that all the brass, all the silver, and all the gold is being brought in for the house of the Lord. These victories are yielding spoil which is going to build the house of the Lord. This is something that David is finding out. Every victory, won corporately or individually, is bringing in precious gifts for the building of the house of God. That is a very real truth. When we are victorious, wherever we are, we are bringing in something to the house of God. God is able to build because of those things. I think it is very important that we should understand that. How much it would encourage us when we are tempted to collapse under the strain of things, when we just simply remember that it is the house of the Lord. Every victory gained is bringing in those vessels of silver, vessels of gold, or much brass, or Hiram who sees David now truly as God's king, sending over carpenters and others and wood in order to help. Well, I think we should learn from all that.

What we have yet to cover, of course, is a very sad part. In a sense, we have come to the end of the happier side of David's rise to the throne and the consolidation of the kingdom. We have now viewed the greatest event of David's reign, which is the capturing of Jerusalem and of it being constituted the city of David and of God, the place where the house of God is to be erected. The ark is brought in as the earnest of the house. The house is to be built and we shall find that the second book of Samuel ends with the purchase of that very threshing floor in Jerusalem which is to be the site of the altar in the very house of God.

But we have yet to view something full of lessons for us: David's sin and then all the consequences that very few of us realise came out of his sin. God forgave him. But oh, what came out of that terrible fall; the last years of David's reign, whilst they were glorious in one way, were filled with conflict and sorrow for himself. So, we will leave that and we will come to it next time.

Shall we just pray together:

Now we place all this into Thy hand, and we ask Thee above and beyond all that has been said, to record in our heart everything, Lord, that was meant for each one of us individually by the Holy Spirit.

There are many situations, many needs, many problems. Lord, use Thy Word to instruct us in Thy ways, and so to bring us to a place where we know the Lord more deeply. We thank Thee for all Thy gracious purpose in bringing us to the throne. But, dear Lord, we know that the throne is, as it were, within Thy house. We ask Thee, Lord, that we will be those given utterly and wholly to Thee first, and then to one another. We ask it in the name of the Lord Jesus. Amen.

4.
David's Sin,
Its Consequences,
and God's Redemption

In II Samuel, chapter 11, we read how David has come to the throne, first of Judah and then of Israel, the whole nation. We have really already reached the heart and meaning of David's life and reign in the preceding chapters. In a sense, from chapter 11 onwards, it is obviously the last years of David's life. Whilst up to now David's life has been filled with conflict and antagonism and suffering, yet it has been really, as it were, like the sun rising. It has just been a steady climb upward. From this point onwards, David's life becomes one of a very different kind of trouble. In a sense, clouds come now into his life, not just around him, but into him.

We have already recognised what is the meaning of David's life and reign. It is summed up in these few chapters just before chapter 11 in three things. One is the capture of Zion and its establishing as the city of God. That is one of *the* greatest things about David's life. There is no doubt about that. Everything about his life has been, as it were, progressively moving toward the capturing and the founding of Zion, forever after to be called David's city and the city of God. All that Jerusalem means in Scripture (and what a lot Jerusalem does mean), in a sense, has come here for the first time into more focused views. Jerusalem, of course, is mentioned once or twice previously, but from this point in the Bible, Jerusalem comes to occupy a central position in God's revelation.

The second great thing about David's reign is that the ark of God has been brought up and has been placed within Zion. There is not only Zion, but the ark of God is in Zion.

The third thing, of course, is the gathering together of material, the making of plans, and the drawing up of plans for the house of God in Zion. This is the heart of David's reign. It is the meaning of his life. It was his vocation. From heaven's point of view, David's life was not the throne, it was this: Zion and the house of God. These were the vocation and the calling of David. But now, having reached the end for which he was brought onto the scene, we are suddenly confronted with David's failure.

Man's Failure after a Great Move of God

Now, this is not so amazing as it may seem. One of the most remarkable things about the record contained in the Bible of the history of humanity is that at each point where some new great move has been made by God with the cooperation of man, immediately after that move is made, the man fails. It is one of the most remarkable facts in Scripture, and indeed it can be carried right through into the New Testament.

Take, for instance, Noah. God takes hold of one man out of all the men of the whole earth. He selects that one man, He trains that one man, He reveals Himself to that one man, and He purposes to make that man a new beginning, a completely new beginning. He wipes out the whole human race and preserves alive that man and his family. As soon as the flood is over, as soon as it is abated, Noah builds an altar. He is told to go out and to re-people the earth and, in the very next paragraph, we find him drunk. What a terrible scene of tragedy and all that came out of that.

Then we can move on to Abraham. We find that as soon as the God of glory appears to Abraham and reveals to him His purpose and all that it means, no sooner is it revealed to him than he fails. Instead of going right into the land, he settles down in Haran. He takes his father, he takes his nephew, he takes other relatives and settles down with them in a halfway halt. When he gets into the land, he is no sooner in the land that God is giving to him and is told to remain in it, than he goes down into Egypt.

You take Moses, another great step in God's economy. At Sinai, God reveals His purpose for His people and the foundation of His dealings with His people, in what we know as the Ten Commandments. As soon as that Law is revealed, and as soon as the covenant is read to the people, the people say, "All these things we will do," and it is ratified by the shedding of blood. The very next paragraph, we find what? They have made them a calf of gold and are worshipping it.

In another great move in God's economy, we find that the tabernacle is revealed, God's dwelling place amongst men. That takes us right up to the end of the book of Exodus. It is revealed in simplicity and yet in detail. Every single part of it is according to the pattern in the heavens. It is the dwelling place of God. No sooner is it revealed, if you move on in the history from Exodus to the book of Numbers and you take up the history again, than it shows the people have completely collapsed. They come right up to the edge of the Jordan. There they reject the Lord, and that generation dies in the wilderness.

Another great move in God's economy is when Joshua takes the whole nation over the Jordan into the land, and they take Jericho. The next minute they come to Ai and they are utterly defeated before the enemy. So, we can go on step after step, each step forward in the economy of God with the cooperation of man. As soon as there has been divine success, man has collapsed.

So, we find it just as true here. As soon as Zion is captured, established as the city of God, the ark is brought in and put in its place, God commits Himself to His people on certain ground, the house of God is coming into view, the materials are being collected, the plans are being drawn up, and then we come face to face with David's failure. That brings us just to this chapter 11 and all that it really holds for us in spiritual lessons.

The Preserving Love of the Lord

What do we really learn from David's failure? Why does the Scripture deal so faithfully and clearly with the sin of David? Because it is here as perhaps our greatest ground of comfort. For whilst, as I have said, all through the history of man, from the beginning of the biblical record, we have found that each time God has done something with a man or through a man, and it has been achieved, that man has failed, God has never withdrawn His grace from that man. He has never forsaken him. He always carries on to the end, punishing His child, His servant, chastening His child, but never forsaking His child, never giving him up to the enemy, never fully as it were, leaving him. So, it is here for our comfort and encouragement and help in all its sordid state. It is written down in the word of God. Every detail about it is plainly put without commentary, that we might draw lessons from it. Not only that we might learn from these lessons how not to fall into the same problem and how to seek the Lord for grace to be preserved, but also, if there be that in which we have failed, to know the grace of God triumphant in a scene of sorrow.

So, I think you will understand a little bit of this part of the history of David. What has it got to do with this wonderful story and record of God's dealings with man in the onward march of His purpose? It is here because this is part and parcel of man. This is the stuff that we are made of. This, if I may put it rather crudely, is the stuff that God has to deal with.

God is the greatest realist in the universe. He is not like us idealists. He is a realist. He does not cry over spilt milk. He comes down to it and from the very condition, the situation, and often the very essence of the problem, He takes hold of those very things that are wrong. Somehow from them and in them, He works out His own wonderful purpose.

There are two Psalms that you ought to go away and read. The first is the 51st Psalm and the second is the 32nd Psalm. These two Psalms were written at this period. You can add others to them if you want to, like the 38th Psalm, which is also written at this period. But the two Psalms that deal with this in the clearest way are Psalm 51 and Psalm 32. Those two wonderful Psalms about contrition, repentance, brokenness, and faith are there for our help and encouragement.

David's Sin and Its Consequences

David Does Not Go Out to Battle

The first thing I want you to note is something I expect we have all heard at one time or another. The root of the matter is found in the simple fact that David tarried at Jerusalem. It says clearly, "... at the time when kings go out to battle ... David tarried at Jerusalem" (II Samuel 11:1). This was the beginning of David's fall. Let us put our finger where the Holy Spirit puts His finger on the fall of David. At the beginning, it was an inward, hidden collapse. David always went out at the head of the army. This is where the trouble began. Somehow or other, as the rabbis have said, David became indulgent. He became somehow or other, more enamoured with the luxuries and comforts of life. He just did not feel like going up. Perhaps, like most of us, he became tired. The battle would be a long, drawn-out one. From his earliest days, he had known nothing but battle, nothing but very real conflict. Now he was crowned king. Now the whole country was, as it were, in peace, in a sense. There had not been a time like it in the history of God's people.

There was an empire for the first time. There was something about Israel now that put it on the footing with the nations. David had got Zion, and the ark of God was in Zion. David was busying himself about the house of God. Somehow, he probably felt tired, and he just did not go out into the battle. He just was not in the forefront of the battle, as many of us so often fall in the same way. Somehow or other, we just get tired and we don't put prayer where it should be put. We don't put the gatherings where they should be put. We don't put our togetherness and other things in the right place. We just find the inward, quiet collapse that begins to take place on the inside.

It comes through weariness and tiredness, strain and pressure and other things of life. David just did not go out to battle when the others went out. That is the first thing I want you to notice. He stayed at Jerusalem. He put himself, without realising it, in the very stream of temptation, with something that was to have the most terrible effect upon his life.

David's Terrible Sin

I want you to notice one or two other things about his terrible sin. We are not going to dwell upon it, but there are one or two things that you should notice. The Scripture puts it down in black and white in all its awfulness.

Uriah stands out in the record as a godly man. Uriah was one of David's 30 great men. In the last part of chapter 23, you will find his name included in the names of the 30. David had the first three, they were called, the second three, and then the 30. These 30 were the greatest, most valiant men in the land. It is believed they had been with him almost from the beginning, from the cave of Adullam. Uriah the Hittite was with David from the beginning. He was a Hittite, and yet he had been converted. He was one who was a foreigner by birth and yet had taken the name of *Jehovah is light*. This shows you something of the background of this man—a godly man, a brave man, a man who had given himself in utter loyalty, first to the Lord and then to God's king and to God's kingdom. Evidently, he had changed his Hittite name for a name like this: the light of the Lord, the Lord is light.

We understand also that he was not only a mighty man in that way, but he had married the daughter of one of his brother captains of the 30. There was another man of the 30 called Eliam. This man's father was Ahithophel, and he had a daughter named Bathsheba. I suppose through Uriah's association with the 30, he came into contact with Eliam's daughter and they were married. Evidently, from what we can gather, the love of Uriah for Bathsheba was proverbial in Jerusalem. It was so proverbial that Nathan could take it up in this little parable that he told David when he said, "There was a poor man who had one little ewe lamb, that was all that he had. And he devoted everything to that one lamb." Thus, we see something in the background of Uriah which only makes this sin stand out in its enormity.

Then, you know what happened when David had taken Bathsheba. The result was only too apparent. David twice tried to cover it up. He brought Uriah back from the battle on the pretence of finding out what was happening on the front line, and then gave him a present and said, "Go home." But without David knowing it, Uriah would not go home. So loyal, so bound up with the interests of God was he, so filled with concern for the interest of the kingdom, that he would only sleep on the doorstep of the king. He would not go out of the threshold of the king's house.

Then, you know, two or three days elapsed, and David brought him in and got him drunk; he tried then to get him to go down to his house. But no, Uriah would not go. Even though he was drunk, he still had that sense of loyalty that made him sleep with the servants of the king. His own words were, "I could not possibly go down to my home when I know that the armies of Israel and Judah are out in the field dwelling in tents and even the ark of God is in a tent." That is the kind of man Uriah was.

The third attempt was the most terrible attempt of all. Without knowing it, Uriah took his own death warrant in his hands. A letter was written by David to Joab telling Joab to put Uriah in the very foremost part of the battle and then to withdraw when the fight was at its highest, so that Uriah would be killed. Uriah had no idea, in his loyalty to his king, that he was carrying the letter which was his own death warrant.

That is the crime of David. It is terrible. I trust that you do not feel that we are being unkind. We are only pointing out to you what is here in the word itself. May it be at least of some help to you to know that the word of God just states clearly, without any commentary, the exact details and facts of the case.

Uriah died. Joab put him at the point where he knew there were the most valiant men of the Ammonites and he died. Then the message was sent back to David saying that some of the mighty men, his mighty men had died, and Uriah the Hittite had also died. Bathsheba spent seven days in mourning and then was taken into the palace. Seven days were the least that she was required to mourn. Then, and this may interest you all, nine months to a year passed without any word at all and without anyone knowing. This should be a tremendous lesson to us all on the silence of God. Some of us, when we do something that is really wrong and we know it is wrong, cannot understand why the Lord is silent. The Lord often is silent. A year goes by without a word of rebuke, without a word of correction, without any exposure, without anything happening. The heavens are silent. Everything goes on as usual.

Nathan Visits David

After a year, when the child is born, Nathan goes into the presence of David and he tells him a parable. Of course, by then no doubt things were a little more distant, although we can tell from the 51st Psalm that David was having a terrible time inwardly. It tells how his bones were, how he felt on his bed, how he had wasted away, how he groaned all night. Why? Because it says, rather amazingly, that he shut it up inside. David knew. For nine months to a year, he hugged his secret to himself and nearly died.

You know what happened when Nathan went into David and told him the story. How David's wrath rose over the man, so that he got up and said, "The man that hath done this is worthy to die: and he shall restore the lamb fourfold, because he did this thing, and because he had no pity."

Nathan said, "Thou art the man."

Then, note this if ever you have to rebuke anyone. Nathan had the wisdom of God. He did not sledgehammer David. He enumerated all the Lord's mercies to David. How the Lord had chosen him, how the Lord had anointed him, how the Lord had made him king, how the Lord had given him a wife, how the Lord would have done such and such, and such and such, if only he had asked, and all the rest of it. Then suddenly he says, why have you done this when the Lord gave you all these things, surrounded you with such grace and provision and deliverance? Why did you do this with Bathsheba? Why did you murder Uriah by the sword of Ammon?

I want you to notice not only the faithfulness of Nathan, but I want you to notice the reaction of David. This is where spiritual character is found out. When we really are found out, we are usually of very few words. When people are wordy and give excuses, you know they don't really mean business. But when they say just a few words, you know that something has gone right home. All David ever said over this terrible matter was, "I have sinned against the Lord." Those were real words. Those were genuine words. They came right out of experience. No excuse, no prevarication, no trying to evade or avoid the issue. It was just simply, "I have sinned against the Lord." As swift as that, the reply came back, "... the Lord has forgiven you. You will not die." The Lord always answers honesty with grace.

So, you have there not only Nathan's faithfulness and David's reaction, but you have the grace of God—utterly forgiven. There are very few of us that would have forgiven in such circumstances. Where one had taken so godly a man, so loyal a man, so trusting a man, so valiant a man, and to have done to him what David did, forgiveness would require a very, very, very great and generous nature. Yet the Lord, in so few words, utterly forgave David.

It is interesting that never again in David's history is it ever flung up in his face by the Lord. When the Lord forgives, He truly forgets. He never again brings it up, ever. It is forgiven—confessed and forgiven.

But then we must learn another lesson, that when we confess truly and say the same things God says about things in our circumstances and lives, when we confess it and God forgives us, we must never make the mistake of thinking that we escape the hand of the Lord. From that point, chastening and scourging begins. Neither is that strange, for if anyone who has in any way failed before the Lord should not know the chastening and the scourging of the Lord, then they are going to lose in the age to come. For we are punished here that we may not be condemned with the world. That is why at the Lord's table, if we have sinned and we partake carelessly, we can either become sick or ill or even die. Why? In order that in being punished in this life, we may escape any condemnation with the world. Now we have to learn this lesson.

Whenever a child of God does something which is really wrong, sins against the Lord, confesses it, and the Lord really forgives, you will never get away from God's punishment, from the chastening that comes in this life, in order that we may escape that which we would have had otherwise. There are a lot of New Testament scriptures which we are going to leave because it is not the subject we are on, but they are there. We are told expressly that we are chastened, we are discriminated against here, that we may not be judged—two different worlds—we may not be judged with the world, not condemned with the world. That is why at one point, you remember, Paul gave someone over to Satan for the destruction of his flesh, that his spirit may be saved in the day of Jesus Christ. What a solemn view that opens up to us of things in this life and in that which is to come.

Well, David is the very example of all that. We find that God's grace forgives utterly and never mentions again his sin. Yet the punishment, the chastening, the scourging begins. First, the child must die, and that will break David's heart. Then the sword will never depart out of David's house in his life, nor from his seed, and how terribly true in his life that became. First, Amnon was murdered, then Absalom was killed, then at his death, Adonijah was killed. Then, right through the history of the house of David, murder after murder in his house. Then he is told the very thing, forgive the word, the lust which has so wrecked David, is that which is going to be found in his own home. It was exactly that, Amnon and Tamar, his stepsister, which brought all the trouble with Absalom. Then later on, you know how his own wives suffered at the hands of Absalom. David suffered through his sin.

David was chastened in his life in a way that gave him an insight into it, gave him an understanding much more than just doing something he wanted to do because suddenly he was taken with a desire. He understood when he saw it happening in others, when he became, as it were, the injured party. He understood then. He understood what was behind it.

Very few of us understand when we sin lightly what it really means, what is the context, the background of it, until we become the injured party. For example, very few of us know the damage we can do with our tongue until we become the injured party. When we become the injured party, we understand the context of the sin, the background of the sin, the harm of the sin, the poison of the sin, and we learn to walk carefully and circumspectly in that matter. That is one thing, but you can take it up in all kinds of things. Do you see what happens? You speak cheaply, easily, harmfully about another and there will come a day when you will be put on the rack by others and you will learn something that you did with your own tongue and its effect and result. You will learn to walk before the Lord. "Before I was afflicted, I went astray; but after I was afflicted, I ran in the way of Thy commands" (see Psalm 119:67).

Let us then remember simply that lesson from David's life. You know how in the last part of chapter twelve we find that the child dies. Let us learn simply from this. Here is the beginning immediately of the chastening of God, that David may be included in the end in God's eternal kingdom and throne. It begins with a child dying. David is absolutely laid out in sorrow. Oh, the suffering of that man! A year passes, a year in which he tried to forget all that he had done. But now the whole thing came back on him, and he relived every moment of those brief hours and days over the murder of Uriah.

Having shown you, I trust, by the grace of God, what comes as a result of our sin, I want to point out a wonderful thing now. We are certainly forgiven utterly of God, yet we suffer by the grace of God at His hand. I want you to notice now the grace of God triumphant. David's child dies, but Bathsheba bears another son and David calls him *peace*. Now, there is something very wonderful about that. That he, after such an experience and at such a point in his life, called one of his children peace is one of the most eloquent testimonies to the grace of God. When a person has no peace, they are wrong with God. Peace is the arbitrator of whether we are in the way of God. David was able to call Solomon *peace*. Nathan called him Jedidiah, *beloved of the Lord*, or *the Lord loved*.

Now, this is all the more wonderful because it is Bathsheba. I will tell you something else which I think is very wonderful. Mary and Joseph have different genealogies. That is the explanation why the genealogy in Matthew is different to the genealogy in Luke, why they do not exactly corroborate each other. One is the genealogy of Mary, the other is the genealogy of Joseph. Both are of the house of David and both are through sons borne by Bathsheba. One comes through Solomon and the other comes through Nathan.

Bathsheba bore four sons in the end. All are mentioned in the record, and two I will mention. Solomon is the first and Nathan is the second. There is something very wonderful about David calling the second one Nathan. He called him the name of the very man that exposed his sin, and that reveals the spiritual character of David. He was able to love the wounds of a faithful friend, able to so love that he was able to call his own son Nathan.

I think it is a wonderful thing that it was Bathsheba who is included in the line of the Messiah, the woman who so sinned. The Messiah came through the couple that fell so deeply. So, it is through her and not through the other wives. It is through her that both Solomon and Nathan are born, both of whom are in the line of the Messiah. So, whether on his father's side or on his mother's side, the Lord is linked with David to Bathsheba.

Well, then you continue in chapters 13 and 14, and you find again all the trouble. You know that in Deuteronomy 17, one thing that Moses said to the children of Israel, when they were just waiting to go over into Jordan, was that when you have a king you must remember certain things. He must not multiply horses, he must not lead you back into Egypt, and he must not multiply his wives. We can trace how every breaking of the commandment of God leads to disorder and to trouble. You know, David was the first king to multiply wives and this was the very thing that was going to be the undoing of Solomon. What he saw and learned in his father's home was to be his own undoing. We can point out how all the trouble in David's house came from the breaking of that simple commandment of the Lord.

Amnon was the eldest son of one of his wives. Absalom and Tamar were the son and the daughter of another. Then of course, there were others, quite a number of others. This is the background of the terrible situation in which Amnon and Tamar and Absalom are found. Amnon developed a very real love for Tamar. The situation—you can read for yourself exactly what happened— but the result was that Absalom was absolutely outraged and swore that he would murder Amnon. Absalom adored his sister Tamar and later on when Absalom had a daughter, he called her Tamar. Then, later on again, you know how he got his own back [revenge] after a year or two—he waited. Then, at the sheep shearing, he invited all the king's sons and they all came. At a certain signal, Absalom's servants slew Amnon and the king's sons fled. Absalom also fled; he had to get out of the country as quickly as possible.

The sword was beginning to work in David's own household. For quite a few years, as you read in chapters 13 and 14, you find that Absalom remains in exile with his father-in-law until at last Joab conceives a very cunning plan. He put the plan into an old woman's heart to go into the king and to pretend that she had a family situation. She goes through it all, speaks to the king about it and asks for his judgment. The king gives his judgment and then she said, "Now, O king, will you allow me to say a few words?"

He said, "Yes."

She said, "Well, what about your son?"

David perceived that he had been trapped and he could do nothing else but call for Absalom to come back—and he did. He wanted Absalom back, but it was a kind of impasse. Joab, who always was a very hard but very far-seeing man, had worked out a plan by which he could break the impasse and bring Absalom back. As you know, Absalom came back but the king would not see him. For quite a few years he remained in Jerusalem, but he never saw David. David would not see him. Then again, Absalom hit on a plan whereby he could get into contact with Joab and, through Joab, get to the king, which he did. Harmony and a reconciliation were restored to the home. Absalom was back.

But Absalom was a striking figure. It is very, very interesting to note how Absalom and his sister Tamar were evidently very striking in physical characteristics. Absalom was absolutely, as it were, the focal point of popularity in Israel. Even more so because he had a very fine state carriage. He had 50 outrunners that ran before it. When he came and went around the country, he was not just a sort of person who lorded it over them. He got down and spoke with them. It says he took their hands and kissed them. It says when he came into the king's palace, he saw, as in oriental palaces, all the folk waiting to go into the king to have cases tried and judged and so on. He used to say to them all, "Oh, dear, what a shame. There is nothing wrong with David, but there is something wrong with the government. They ought to appoint someone like me to deal with all you folk. Then we would get justice done. We would get things done more quickly." It says simply that he stole the hearts of the people. They all said, "He is a fine fellow, Absalom. He is not afraid to talk with us. He is not afraid to come down to us. He seems fair; he seems just."

It says, after four years, Absalom asked leave of David. Could he go to Hebron? He had made a vow. David said that of course he could go. They took 200 men, and it says they went in the simplicity of their heart. Those 200 men did not know what was up. They went in the simplicity of their hearts. Division always begins like that. It begins quietly, slowly, with all the outward looks and legality, legitimacy. It always seems to have much behind it and much for it. It seems always to be very fair and just. Generally, people are carried away into it and with it because of the simplicity of their hearts.

But the secret word had gone out throughout Israel. "When the trumpet sounds in Hebron, rally to Absalom, for he will be king." Then you know what happened. The trumpet sounded. Read from 15 onwards and we find the trumpet certainly does sound, and the people are in a state of absolute disorder. No one knows where to turn or what to do.

Then we enter into perhaps the deepest lesson of David's life and one of our greatest lessons, if we can but learn it. David decides that there is no point in staying in Jerusalem and trying to defend it. They will only raze it to the ground. He decides the only way out is to flee. In this, David once again shows himself to be a man after God's own heart, whatever his failure. From the very beginning to the end, David has never taken any kind of action to either get onto the throne or to keep the throne. One of the most remarkable characteristics about David has been the way that, when the throne was right in his hand—he could have had it—he refused to take any action at all. When he was on it, he refused in any way to condone the murder of his rival, Ish-bosheth, when he was murdered. Or Abner, his arch enemy, when he was murdered, it says, he went behind his bier weeping.

David always refused in any way either to try and get the throne, or to hold the throne, or in any way to keep people down. His attitude was that if the Lord, who had brought him to the throne, was not going to keep him on the throne, then David was in the hands of the Lord for whatever the Lord wanted. Oh, let us always learn that lesson. Never take on defection. Never take on division. Do not come down to the roundtable conversation. Do not try to thrash the thing out. You will never get anywhere. If God has any place for you, then just learn the deepest lesson you can learn: that if God has a place for you, He will not only get you into that place, but God will keep you in that place whether you are driven out or not.

David was driven out. As always (and this is another bitter lesson some of us, if not all of us, have to learn in our lives), when you are kicked, everyone who has any axe to grind will kick you and will kick you hard. It is only when you are down that you find out your real friends and your false friends—only then. You never know until you are down. It is absolutely remarkable the way in which the Holy Spirit draws out all the friends of David, all these people who had given lip service. All these people who had been in the court, all these people who had been in the kingdom. Now what happens? Ah, you find many have gone over to Absalom. Many now are talking in very superior tones about David. "Oh, who is David? What is David?"

You find some are prepared to go out with David. Here is one of the most wonderful lessons we can learn in these chapters.

Ittai the Gittite is a Philistine. David says to him, "Why do you come out with me?"

Ittai says, "Wherever you go, wherever you die, I'm coming and I'm dying. Don't you tell me to go away." David had found out a real friend.

There were some who were prepared to stay in the city. There were others who were prepared to go out into the wilderness and die with David, be annihilated with David. They were going to go. The 600 went out with him. The 600 had been with him from the beginning. In spite of the fact that obviously by then they knew what had happened to Uriah the Hittite, they were sticking with God's king. Out they went together.

Then you find Hushai the Archite. He comes, an aged man. But you find that he is going to absolutely stay with David. David says, "Go back into Jerusalem and confound the council of Ahithophel." Ahithophel had been David's closest counsellor, his greatest, eldest statesman. He had relied upon him in every way. Ahithophel was the grandfather of Bathsheba. He had an axe to grind, something that was nagging the back of his heart. He was behind Absalom and with Absalom. David said to Hushai, "Go in and confound the council of Ahithophel."

Then you find others. You find people who will go with you into exile but are only with you for what they can gain. Ziba comes and he tells a lie about Mephibosheth, Jonathan's son, saying he went over to Absalom the moment it was heard. He said, "Ah, I'll go to Absalom. I might get the throne back," which was a lie. David said to Ziba, "Very well. All that belongs to Mephibosheth shall be yours when the kingdom is restored." But Ziba was a liar.

Then, of course, there is the story of Shimei. It always makes us smile. As David went up the Mount of Olives, it says Shimei ran up and down on the other side of the ravine, casting up dust, throwing stones at him. You know that kind of thing, taking up stones and throwing them. "You man of blood," he kept on yelling across the ravine. "You man of blood. Now all the judgments ..." and he went through them all, all the judgments—Abner and Ish-Bosheth and Saul. He blamed the lot on David. He swore and he cursed him.

Abishai said, "Let me go over that ravine and take that man's head off." He said, "Why should you let a dead dog speak to you like that?"

But David said to him, and again it revealed spiritual character, "Let him curse me. Let him curse me. The Lord has bidden him to curse me. If I am suffering from a son that came out of my own bowels, how much more can I bear something from someone who is a Benjaminite?" So, it says they went on and Shimei threw up a bit more dust and cast a few more stones. It was humiliating.

Well, that's the story of Absalom's rebellion. You know what happened, how, in the end, when the battle closed in, Absalom's mule went under a very large terebinth in the forest. He had very long hair, and his head got caught in the branches and tangled and thus he swung there. So, Joab went and pushed three sharpened staves through his body. Then ten soldiers finished him off and he was buried. That was the end of Absalom. Yet before all Israel, here is another wonderful point of spiritual character. As the armies went out through the gates, David had been told to remain. He wanted to go out with them, but they said, "No, you must not." As each captain went by, he just said, "Gently, for my sake, with Absalom." That is just what it is literally, *gently for my sake with Absalom.* It says that the whole of the host of Israel heard David's command to the captains.

I suppose most of you must have, at one time or another, read the story of Absalom's death and David's reaction in chapter 18. But I don't believe (and this is a thing I think we should take account of) this could have been written by anyone else but an eyewitness. This must have been one document that was written by an eyewitness. Because, you know, when people come to write up things like this, they always gloss them over and they make them much more flowery. But in actual fact, you know, when those runners came into David, he had been watching and waiting, and waiting and watching. The first word the man said was, "Peace."

The first word David said was, "Is there peace with Absalom?"

When they said, "No, Absalom is dead," you have just got the picture of a man struck speechless with grief. All that comes out of him is just over and over and over again, "My son, my son Absalom, my son." All the time. It is obviously an eyewitness account of what happened. Anyone else who would have written about it years afterwards would have certainly made it a little more flowery.

Then, you know how at last they all come back and they want to finish off Shimei. But David says, "No, you mustn't do that. You just leave him," and the others who had part in the rebellion. He would not let them do it. He stood for peace on every side. The thing that stands out is what David said to the two high priests as they took back the ark of the Lord. He said, "If the Lord does not delight in me, all well and good; I am in the hand of the Lord." That, I think, takes a lot of faith. In other words,

David said, "If I am to die at the hand of Absalom and this insurrection because the Lord has finished with me, very well. I do not want to live if it is not in the purpose and the will and the favour of God." That shows you the kind of man that David was. In spite of sin, his heart was for the Lord.

Then in chapter 20, there is simply yet another insurrection by a man called Sheba. He is just called a worthless, a base fellow, as it says in this version, and there is another rebellion. David's closing years are filled with all this kind of strife and trouble. That brings you really to the end of the history, as far as these two books of Samuel go.

The Appendix–Characteristics of Kingship

Chapters 21, 22, 23, and 24 are an appendix. They are just four appendices. One deals with an incident at the very beginning of David's reign as king. The last one deals with an incident at the end of his reign as king. In other words, these four appendices, I am quite sure, are here by the placing of the Holy Spirit as a kind of summary of the salient characteristics of kingship.

Divine Government of God

What are they? The first in chapter 21 has caused a lot of people a lot of trouble. How on earth can the Lord require seven fellows to be hanged? But in actual fact, the story is not as simple as that. Saul waged a terrible warfare on the Gibeonites. The Gibeonites had a covenant, a pact, with the children of Israel for every generation. It was a pact forever that they would never be touched, but would be allowed to be servants to the people of God in all generations. Saul dismissed that and, evidently, with his sons, waged a terrible warfare of annihilation. You can find it here in these verses: to destroy them out of the borders of Israel (see v. 5). Everyone had forgotten the covenant that had been made with Gibeon. No one read the word of God and found out about it. Everyone forgot. But there was a famine which lasted three years. David's first reaction when there was trouble was to get on his knees and to seek the face of the Lord.

That is one of the salient characteristics of kingship, the government of God—direct government. He did not decide what he was going to do. He did not decide what was wrong. He did not decide what the answer was. He got on his knees, and he asked the Lord, and the Lord showed him clearly what was wrong. The answer was that those who had perpetrated such deeds would have to pay the price. In those days, they asked for the sons of the man that perpetrated it.

David sought out the seven and handed them over to them. They were first killed. Then, as was the custom, their bodies were hung up and they were left. From the beginning of the barley harvest, right through the summer, they were left. The mother of two of them, it says, stayed there all the way through those months, sleeping there in a tent under them, and in the day, frightening off the vultures. It is a terrible, terrible picture. But the awful deeds perpetrated by Saul and his sons were avenged. It says the land was healed and the Philistines were defeated. The key to this is that David got on his knees and sought the face of the Lord.

Next, and this is interesting, you get two Psalms of David. The first one in chapter 22 was written just after he came to the throne, and the second one was his dying work. As you have one incident at the beginning of his reign and one incident in chapter 24 at the end of his reign, so you have one Psalm which is the beginning of his reign and one which contained his actual last words. What does this Psalm reveal? It reveals a man with a deep, intimate, inwrought, and utterly dependent experience of the Lord.

The Heart of Kingship

You will never find any Psalm in Scripture that uses so many titles for the Lord, that calls the Lord so many things: my defence, my rock, my high tower, my shield, my strength, my everything. David was simply sharing right out of his heart, how he had come to the throne, because the Lord was his everything. That is the heart of kingship. He did not get there himself, he came there by the grace of God. He learned to know the Lord in a very deep way. For it says in one place that when he was in distress, he called the Lord. The Lord came to him in a storm, in a way that frightened him, in a way that, as it were, would seem as if the end had come—but it was the answer of God. It was God answering him. That is how the Lord really answered him there. You find that he attributes everything to Him: the way he leaps over a rampart, the way his arms can bend a bow of brass. He attributes everything to the Lord. He says, "By the Lord, I do these things." You see, he had come to find that the Lord was the key to everything. The Lord was the provision for everything. The Lord was the heart of it all.

The Mighty Men of David

Then in the last part of chapter 23, you will find the mighty men of David named. The first three, the second three, and the 30. Actually, there were 31 in the 30, but the name of that band was "the 30." These were the mighty men of David. What do we learn from that? They learned simply that in God's kingdom, we only come and get to the throne in fellowship. These were tremendous men. In Chronicles, you will find recorded what they did. They slew bears in the time of snow, they swam rivers, they killed so many at one time, and so on. They were true mighty men. If these were some of the mighty men, I don't know what the not so mighty men were like by our standards.

There is something very wonderful in that about God's kingdom. The first three, the second three, and the 30. And then the people. I wonder whether that is not a picture of what, one day, the kingdom is going to be like when we get there. We shall find that there is the congregation, the people of God. We shall find that there are the 30, we shall find there are the second three, we shall find there are the first three. Then we shall find the King. So we learn all those things.

Divine Government and Authority

Lastly, in chapter 24, you have again another incident which reveals to us the character of David. There is a plague. Something happens. David numbers the people, and there is a plague. What this reveals to us is very simple. What would you have done? What would you have done if you had been responsible for this tragedy amongst the people of God and in the work of

God? If the Lord said to you, "I will give you three choices: seven years famine, three months exile, or three days' plague." I wonder what you would have said. I wonder whether you would have said, "three days plague," and you would have been found out.

That revealed spiritual character. David said, "Lord, I would not choose. I am in your hand. If you think seven years famine is what is necessary because of my sin, I am in your hand." That reveals spiritual character, and that is the heart of kingship. From beginning to end, it is summed up like that. David said, from beginning to end, "I am in the hands of the Lord." As far as the throne was concerned in the days of Saul, as far as the throne was concerned when he was on it, as far as the throne was concerned when he fell, he was in the hands of the Lord. So, the Lord sent a plague on Israel. And the last paragraph from the books of Samuel says:

> *And Gad came that day to David, and said unto him, Go up, rear an altar unto Jehovah in the threshing-floor of Araunah the Jebusite. And David went up according to the saying of Gad, as Jehovah commanded. And Araunah looked forth, and saw the king and his servants coming on toward him: and Araunah went out, and bowed himself before the king with his face to the ground. And Araunah said, Wherefore is my lord the king come to his servant? And David said, To buy the threshing-floor of thee, to build an altar unto Jehovah, that the plague may be stayed from the people. And Araunah said unto David, Let my lord the king take and offer up what seemeth good unto him: behold, the oxen for the burnt-offering, and the threshing instruments and the yokes of the oxen for the*

wood: all this, O king, doth Araunah give unto the king. And
Araunah said unto the king, Jehovah thy God accept thee. And
the king said unto Araunah, Nay; but I will verily buy it of
thee at a price; neither will I offer burnt-offerings unto Jehovah
my God which cost me nothing. So David bought the threshing-
floor and the oxen for fifty shekels of silver. And David built
there an altar unto Jehovah, and offered burnt-offerings and
peace-offerings. So Jehovah was entreated for the land, and
the plague was stayed from Israel. II Samuel 24:18–25

The plague was stayed. But this is a far, far greater thing, as we shall find in the book of Kings. That threshing floor is the site of the house of God.

This is just like the Lord. This is one of the greatest lessons of David. David falls with and through Bathsheba. Very well—the Lord will take Bathsheba and will make her mother of Solomon, will make her a link in the chain, in the seed, the royal line of the Messiah.

David fell, and there was a plague. Very well. Through that plague, through that terrible, terrible punishment, David will purchase the very site which is going to be the dwelling place of God. Let us take encouragement from that—not to be loose, not to be lax, but to remember. Let us remember that even when we fail, and we do fail, and even when we sin against the Lord, when there is real contrition and genuineness and confession, the Lord takes the very things that caused our fall and makes them the very things to fulfil His purpose concerning them and concerning Himself.

May the Lord just teach us that.

Study Guide

We need to remember that in the Hebrew, I and II Samuel form one book. The Septuagint treats them along with I and II Kings as "The Four Books of the Kingdom." The Vulgate also groups I and II Samuel with Kings and calls them "The Four Books of the Kings." It is in fact, a complete history of the kingdom in four sections.

In I and II Samuel, we have come to a completely new phase in the history of God's people. God has taken another great step forward. It is almost true to say that we have here a new beginning of God. We are now to see the people of God established as the Kingdom of God, under the guidance of the word of God. Two new things come into being through Samuel—the prophetic order and the monarchy.

It is instructive from the earliest days these books should have been called by Samuel's name, when seemingly they deal more with other people. In each new beginning of God we have found a man—Abraham, then Moses, and now Samuel. All three are pioneers. Samuel himself is the last of the Judges, and the first of the long line of prophets. He, in a variety of ways, was to influence Israel for generations. In fact, he was a great turning point in the Old Testament. He combined in himself all the Old Testament offices, priesthood, prophecy and kingship. He was both a Levite and a Nazirite. We believe it was Samuel who first instituted "the schools of the prophets" which were to affect the nation culturally, educationally, and spiritually.

We have seen already in Ruth how the Lord has worked sovereignly to provide a king. The book of Ruth ends with a king. Now we go back again to see how God prepares and appoints the instrument by which the kingdom is to be brought in.

Especial Note: Background History

The period of history which these books cover is, by and large, the period to which succeeding generations always looked back with nostalgia. Indeed, forever after, the Jewish people were to look for another "David."

The establishment of the kingdom came at a time when both Egypt and Assyria, the super-powers of the day, were passing through a state of comparative weakness.

First Samuel covers the period of history during which the Canaanite tribes were finally subdued. The Philistine settlements, however, along the coast had so increased in strength that they presented a continual threat of invasion to Israel. This called for strong, courageous, spiritually able leadership and for the uniting of the people.

Second Samuel records the period when the Hebrew monarchy reached its golden age. David unified the nation, founded the capital at Jerusalem, subdued all enemies and founded the dynasty which has inspired the people of God throughout all subsequent generations. It was during David's reign that music and poetry were considerably developed, as was public administration (see II Samuel 8:10–17.) Most, if not all, of these matters were to become the basic constituents in the life, worship and thinking of the people of God, e.g. David's throne, the Kingdom, the Davidic line (Messiah), Jerusalem, Zion, the house of God, the Psalms, the very language of the Psalms, etc.

Authorship and Date

The author is not clearly indicated, but it is abundantly clear that the book was compiled from various authorities. (See I Samuel 10:25, I Chronicles 29:29, II Samuel 1:18.) Certainly Samuel, Nathan, and Gad wrote much of it. There is much to suggest that some of the sources were eyewitnesses of what they recorded.

The two books cover a century of history approximately, from Eli to the accession of Solomon, and were probably written in their present form during the reign of Rehoboam, 930–914 BC. They were certainly written after David's death and not earlier than the division of the nation into two – into Northern and Southern kingdoms (I Samuel 27:6.) There has been much controversy over the authorship and date of I and II Samuel involving many complex theories. The language in which they are written suggests an early date, i.e. somewhere near the beginning of the division.

Key to the Book

The key to these books is undoubtedly "The King, Kingdom and Kingship." We find that "Kingship" is clearly the meaning and end of Samuel's life and work. In Saul's life this matter is revealed negatively, and in David's life, positively. In fact, in general terms we could say that in I Samuel we see a king after man's thinking, resulting in tragedy, and in II Samuel we see a king after God's own heart, leading to glory.

In I and II Samuel we are not given merely a chronological order of events, nor are we given pure biography as such. Facts are either included or excluded, according to the aim of the books—God's King and God's Kingdom.

One thing which we see clearly is David as the type of Christ, God's King. We see also the divine concept of a kingdom. The fact is that this kingdom, frail and human, which came in with David, is a foreshadowing of the kingdom of God. From the history of this kingdom we begin to learn the deep principles of kingship to which all who have been saved are called by the grace of God. (See Revelation 1:6; and 5:10.) David's way to the throne is the way every believer must come to the throne of God. (See Revelation 3:21; 2:26 and II Timothy 2:12.) There is no other way to "reign," or to have "authority." This matter is not a question of office or outward trappings, or titles. It is a matter of deep inward spiritual character, experience, and history with God.

Note also that the house of God, the temple, was the one expression of David's life. (See Psalm 27:4–6; compare to Psalm 132:1–5. Psalm 23:6; I Chronicles 28:2.) Hidden at first, it becomes more and more apparent, until the last chapter of II Samuel brings us to the purchase of the site, and setting up of an altar, upon which site the temple was later to be built by Solomon. The reign of David as king led to the building of the temple. This is not only true of Christ as King (Matthew 16:18); it is true surely of those He saves and calls. Has the church ever been founded, or built up, except by the authority and power of the risen Christ through His own? (See Matthew 16:19.)

Outline of the Book

The Instrument to Bring in God's King and Kingdom: I Samuel 1–16:13

A. The producing of that instrument: I Samuel 1:1–3:18

i. The evil days of Eli and his sons: I Samuel 2:12–3:6

ii. Elkanah (God acquired) and Hannah (grace)

    a) The Lord shut up the womb: I Samuel 1:5–6

    b) Suffering and travail: I Samuel 1:10

    c) An attitude forged: I Samuel 1:11, 15, 19

    d) Samuel born: I Samuel 1:20

iii) A new phase in God's economy opens

    a) Wholly given: I Samuel 1:27–28

    b) God's "need" and Hannah's need

    c) His service begins with a burnt offering: I Samuel 1:24

    d) Hannah's song of triumph and praise: I Samuel 2:1–11

iv) The calling of Samuel: I Samuel 3:1–18

B. The development of that instrument: I Samuel 3:19–8:1

i. The Word of God by Samuel: I Samuel 3:19; I Samuel 4:1, compare to I Samuel 3:1

ii. The ark captured, death of Eli, his sons and daughter-in-law: 1 Samuel 4

iii. The ark among the Philistines: 1 Samuel 5

iv. The beginning of Samuel's reformation: 1 Samuel 7:1–4

v. Samuel's circuit: 1 Samuel 7:15 Bethel, Gilgal, Mizpah, Ramah

vi. A long life of ministry unrecorded: 1 Samuel 7:15–8:

In the succeeding chapters, it is Samuel whom God uses to bring the kingdom.

II. The Principles of Kingship. Saul and David
1 Samuel 8:1–II Samuel 1:27

A. The way in which the kingdom was introduced 1 Samuel 8:1–22

i. The false and the true kingdom vv. 7–9. God wanted to give them a king, although the impression given is that the basis upon which the people requested a king was false. They wanted a king in order to be like the world. Their motive was wrong. Upon that basis the true kingdom could not be built. Indeed, God gave them the kind of man they wanted. It was false from its origin to its end.

ii. We must note, therefore, the way in which in these chapters the false and true are contrasted.

iii. The people's request for a king vv 4–5

iv. Samuel's heart brokenness—the people's motive—"like all the nations" v6, compare to v5.

B. Saul—the natural choice of the natural man

i. He had many very good qualities: 1 Samuel 9:2, 4, 21; 10:16, 21, 22; 11:13

ii. Saul and the things of God: 1 Samuel 10:1, 10, 26; 11:6, 15; 14:33, 35, 47, 48; 15:31

iii. Saul's disobedience

a) The sacrifice: 1 Samuel 13

b) The Amalekites: 1 Samuel 15

iv. Saul and fellowship in God's work 1 Samuel 10:26; 11:7; 14:5

v. Saul's murderous jealousy and his end 1 Samuel 18:8–13, 22–25; 19:9–11; 20:30–34; 1 Samuel 28–31

vi. Note: the ease and facility with which he came to the throne— no satanic opposition

C. David—the man after God's heart

i. The shepherd boy: 1 Samuel 16–17

a) Note 1 Samuel 16:14-23, compare to 17:12; 17:55. Why the seeming discrepancy? Was the writer or compiler looking back to David's earlier life, and tracing a spiritual history? Certainly, the story of Goliath reveals that David had already a life with the Lord.

b) 1 Samuel 16:18: Skilful in playing; a mighty man of valour, a man of war; prudent in speech; a comely person; the Lord was with him. These qualities did not suddenly develop overnight. It required discipline and training. For example, to be an accomplished musician does not only require gift but much discipline and training. The same with being an accomplished athlete and warrior. Note Psalm 18:29–35.

c) 1 Samuel 17:26, 37, and 45–47: this reveals an experiential knowledge, which David already had. He had experienced and proved the Lord in his daily routine life. Note Psalm 23, traditionally placed in his early years.

ii. David in Saul's household and service: 1 Samuel 18:1–19:7

1 Samuel 18:8, 9, 20, 29, compare to 18:5, 14, 30 all David's previous experience was now put to the test in Saul's household and service. Note Ahimelech's words later spoken, 1 Samuel 22:14 "who ... is so faithful as David," also 1 Samuel 18:14, "David behaved himself wisely."

iii. David, the fugitive: 1 Samuel 19:8–II Samuel 1

a) If David's previous experience had been tried in Saul's service, the acid test came in the long years of being a fugitive and an exile. Many times David could have taken the matter of becoming king into his own hands, and could have argued that he had been anointed by Samuel.

b) Saul had been unable to wait for even a few days for Samuel; David had to wait many years. Patience in the work of God, that quality of steadfast endurance, is the thing which finds us all out as to spiritual character. The flesh can never wait even in the things of God.

c) Naoith – with Samuel: 1 Samuel 19:8–24

d) Ezel – with Jonathan: 1 Samuel 20:1–42

e) Nob – the Tabernacle: 1 Samuel 21:1–9

f) Gath – the Philistines: 1 Samuel 21:10–15

g) Adullam – the 400: 1 Samuel 22

h) Hachilah – keilah: 1 Samuel 23
(Treachery, shallowness, politics)

i) Engedi—Abigail—hachilah: 1 Samuel 24–26
(Vindication, vengeance, taking advantage)

j) Ziklag—the Philistines: 1 Samuel 27–31
A gift.

k) Saul's death: 1 Samuel 28–31

iv. David crowned king: II Samuel 1–2

a) The crowning of David really belongs to the next division, but it is good for us to underline the fact here.

b) In David's lament over both Saul and Jonathan, we see the kind of man he was. See II Samuel 1. He is a man "pure in heart," and of a "contrite spirit." Jonathan had done nothing but good to David, but Saul only evil. His lament over Jonathan is understandable, but over Saul it is remarkable.

c) Thus it was by conflict, by suffering, by self-revelation, through inwrought experience of life in every way, and above all, by a deep heart knowledge of God, and an utter dependence upon Him, that God's man came to the throne; There is no other character to kingship, and no other way to the throne.

III. The Establishment of the Kingdom: II Samuel 2:20

A. David at Hebron: II Samuel 2:1–5:5

i. Hebron—a *ford*, a *company*, signifies fellowship

ii. David was crowned there as King of Judah: II Samuel 2:1–7

iii. The division of the nation—Judah and Israel: II Samuel 2:8–4:12 (Joab—Abner—Ishbosheth)

iv. David finally crowned king of Israel: II Samuel 5:1–5

B. David at Jerusalem: II Samuel 5:6–10:19

i. Zion captured—the city of God: II Samuel 5:6–25

A brilliant military exploit, but nevertheless achieved by faith in God. This could have been done by Joshua. See Joshua 15:63, compare to Joshua 1:3. Thus there was a 400 year lapse between the promise given, and the condition fulfilled, and promise inherited. From this point on Zion and Jerusalem became the capital of the nation, the focal point of the life and worship of God's people. It becomes the main symbol of God's eternal purpose for man, His desire to dwell among us.

ii. The ark brought up to Zion: II Samuel 6:1–2

The ark symbolises the presence of the Lord. Thus we see the Lord committing Himself to Zion. Note Uzzah's presumption. "The fear of the Lord is the beginning of wisdom." See Psalm 111:10; Acts 5:1–6; I John 5:16. Note also that the ark was always to be carried on the shoulders of the priests, never by mechanical means. See Numbers 4:15; I Chronicles 15:2, 13, the presence of the Lord is committed always to people, not to things. The natural mind makes many mistakes over this in the work and service of God.

iii. David's desire to build the house of God, and the Lord's reaction: II Samuel 7:1–29

This chapter reveals the lifelong passion of David's heart. He had seen something of the eternal purpose of God, and this gave rise to his desire to build the Lord's house in Jerusalem. This is expressed in many of his Psalms. In fact, David was not allowed to build the house, although all the materials for it were gathered by him, the money collected through him, and the plans drawn up under him.

iv. The Lord's covenant with David: II Samuel 7:1–29

This is really all to do with "great David's greater Son." It was the promise that David's line would last until the coming of the Messiah. Then that throne and kingdom would be forever. Here rises one of the major themes of the Bible–the throne and line of David. The Messianic line has now become the Davidic line.

It might be helpful to trace the prophecies concerning the Messiah as they relate to this matter:

Genesis 3:15	Given approx 4000 BC	Seed of the Woman
Genesis 9:26	Given approx 2300 BC	Shem
Genesis 12:1–3, 7	Given approx 2000 BC	Abraham
Genesis 26, 3–4	Given approx 1800 BC	Isaac
Genesis 28:13–14		Jacob
Genesis 49:10		Judah
II Samuel 7: 11–17	Given approx 1000 BC	

Comparing the genealogies in Matthew 1:1–16 and Luke 3:23–38, we discover that Mary is descended from David through Nathan, and Joseph through Solomon.

v. David's victories over all his enemies provide the material for the building of the Lord's house: II Samuel 8:1–10:19. This has much to teach us.

C. David's sin and its consequences: II Samuel 11:1–20:28

Note: We have already reached the heart and meaning of David's reign and life in the past few chapters. Zion is the city of God; the ark is already there; the materials for the Lord's house are being gathered and prepared. Then, suddenly, we are confronted with David's failure and its consequences. This is remarkably true of the whole history of man as recorded in the Bible, e.g. Adam, Noah, Abraham, the Sinai Covenant, the Tabernacle, Joshua and Jericho, etc. Above all, we see the faithfulness, the mercy, and the preserving love of the Lord.

i. David does not go out to battle: II Samuel 11:1

He was not where he should have been. In such small ways, great and terrible falls come.

ii. David's terrible sin: II Samuel 11:2–27

Greater than David's sin with Bathsheba is his sin against Uriah. It was premeditated murder.

iii. The prophet Nathan's visit. David's reaction and God's supreme grace: II Samuel 12:1–15

iv. The child dies in spite of David's sorrow and fasting. Both Solomon (Jedidiah) and Nathan are born of Bathsheba: II Samuel 12:15–31

v. Amnon, Tamar, Absalom: II Samuel 13–14

vi. Absalom's rebellion: II Samuel 15–19

vii. Sheba's rebellion: II Samuel 20

An Appendix. II Samuel 21–24

We ought to note that this appendix commences and concludes with essentially the same lesson in two different incidents, one from the beginning of his reign and one at the end. Both incidents teach us much about divine government and authority.

I. Divine Government and Authority:
II Samuel 21

Famine and the reason for it. The Gibeonites and their request. The defeat of the Philistines. The key: David sought the Lord's face. He did not have authority in himself or apart from God.

II. The Heart of Kingship:
II Samuel 22:1–23:7

These two Psalms, one written before David fell, and the other his last words, reveal the essential character of kingship, according to God. Note how they reveal a deep, intimate, inwrought experience of the Lord. They are the words of a man whose very life is God. He is utterly dependent on upon the Lord. This is the key to true authority.

III. The mighty men of David:
II Samuel 23:8–39

They are divided into three groups—the first three, the second three, and the thirty (actually there were thirty-one.) These men in fellowship with David executed the will of God and became the vehicle for the mighty acts of God. At the heart of the kingdom was a group of men in living fellowship.

IV. Divine government and authority:
II Samuel 24

The numbering of the people and David's remorse. The actual numbering of the people in itself was not the sin. See Numbers 1:2; 26:1–2. It must have been David's motive for numbering the people that was wrong. See verses 2 and 3. The word of the Lord by Gad, the prophet and David's reaction. Mark how David leaves it to the Lord to decide (again we have a key to true authority.) The plague and resulting death. Note carefully that when David confesses his sin, and asks the Lord to act against him, rather than the people, the Lord turns the whole matter into a blessing, The Lord reveals to David the site for the building of the temple, his lifelong desire. Note verse 18 and 19: without the cross, there can be no building of God's house.

Message of the Book

The way to the throne is an exceedingly difficult and hard one. It requires a deep, inwrought experience and spiritual history. All self-interest and self-strength must be broken. We can only ever come to the throne through absolute dependence upon the Lord and by costly dealings with Him. Nevertheless, His grace is wonderfully sufficient and never fails. He can even take our most painful and dark falls, once they have been truly confessed, and use them as stepping stones to the fulfillment of His purpose.

Recommended Books:

Israel under Samuel, Saul and David to the birth of Solomon
A. Edersheim

David
F.B. Meyer

David
J. Hercus

Samuel the Prophet
F.B. Meyer

Study Guide Questions

1. State briefly in your own words what is the main thing that we see God doing in I & II Samuel.

2. Describe, in about two paragraphs, the position and importance of Samuel and his work to the thing that we see God doing in I & II Samuel.

3. Answer the following, each in a single sentence:
a) What was the condition of the priesthood in Israel when Samuel was a child?

b) What was the condition of the monarchy in Israel just before David came to power?

c) What was the state of the nations surrounding Israel before Saul came to power?

d) Why did Israel want to have a king, and what was the reaction of the Lord to this?

4. In I and II Samuel we find man choosing a king, and we find God choosing a king. What do you think were the main faults in the king chosen by man?

5. What do the following verses teach you about authority on earth, which God honours?
a) I Samuel 13:13–14

b) I Samuel 16:13–18

c) I Samuel 23:2, 4 and 10–13

d) I Samuel 24:6; II Samuel 1:14–16

e) I Samuel 30:6–8

f) II Samuel 2:1–4

g) II Samuel 5:17–25

h) II Samuel 8:15 cf Hebrews 1:9

i) II Samuel 22:21–35, 51

j) II Samuel 23:2–5

Do these lessons help you to fulfill God's plan for your life as shown in Romans 5:17; II Timothy 2:12?

6. Write about half a page, describing events in David's early life which helped to train him for the position and work which God had prepared for him.

7. What do you learn about David's great passion and burden from the following passages?
a) II Samuel 6:2, 12–19

b) II Samuel 7:1–29

c) II Samuel 24:15–25, compare to II Chronicles 3:1

Does this burden remind you of Matthew 16:18?

8. Write a few sentences on each of the following women:
a) Hannah

b) Abigail

c) Michal

d) The woman in 1 Samuel 28:6–25

e) Bathsheba

9. Write a few sentences about each of the following men:
a) Eli

b) Jonathan

c) Hushai

d) Absalom

e) Joab

f) Uzzah

g) Mephibosheth

h) Nathan

10. Examine the following passages. Do they speak to you in anyway about the Lord Jesus Christ?

a) I Samuel 18:1–5

b) I Samuel 30:1–31

c) I Samuel 5:10

d) II Samuel 8:1–15

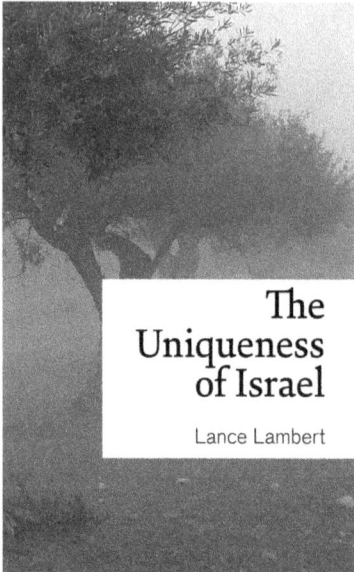

The Uniqueness of Israel

Woven into the fabric of Jewish existence there is an undeniable uniqueness. There is bitter controversy over the subject of Israel, but time itself will establish the truth about this nation's place in God's plan. For Lance Lambert, the Lord Jesus is the key that unlocks Jewish history He is the key not only to their fall, but also to their restoration. For in spite of the fact that they rejected Him, He has not rejected them.

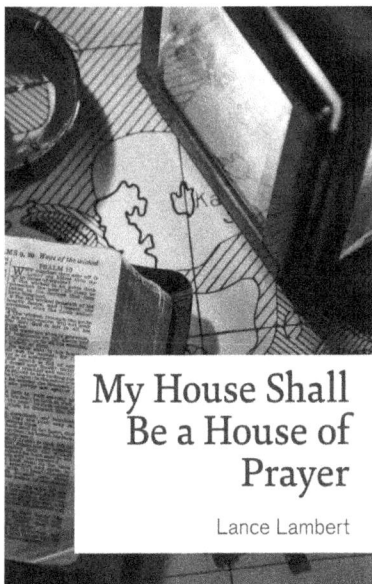

My House Shall Be a House of Prayer

As the return of the Lord draws near there has never been a time when effective prayer is more strategic, necessary, and essential than now. Will we be a people who will truly watch and pray? Will anyone respond to His call and challenge? Corporate intercession is almost a lost art—and that when we most need it!

> *I sought for a man among them, that should build up the wall, and stand in the gap before me for the land, that I should not destroy it; but I found none (Ezekiel 22:30).*

This is the call and challenge of the Lord.

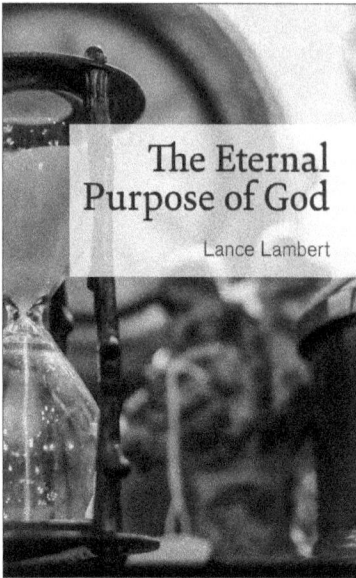

The Eternal Purpose of God

There is no truth that is of greater importance than this matter of God's eternal purpose. Once you begin to understand God's ultimate aim in time, and for the ages to come, life becomes more meaningful and significant. Why did God create this universe and this earth, which at our present extent of knowledge is unique? What was His aim and goal in its creation? Why did He create mankind? And when man fell short of His glory through sin, why did He persevere and provide salvation? Is that salvation an end in itself, or is it a means to an end, with everything provided within it to reach the final goal? And how can I be involved in the fulfillment of that purpose?

This book is a helpful response to these questions, revealing the heart of God.

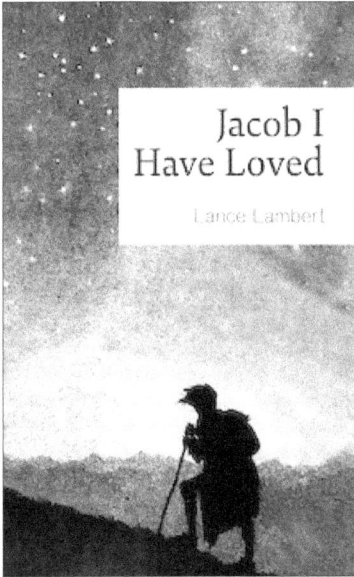

Jacob I Have Loved

When God deals with us it is often in deeply mystifying ways. There is no greater example of how God shapes a person than through the remarkable story of Jacob. It is an outstanding illustration of God's desire to utterly transform our fallen inner nature. Despite a twisted, deceiving, and sinful heart, Jacob nonetheless inherited God's richest blessings and became one of the patriarchs of our faith. Herein lies one of the Bible's great mysteries. The amazing truth is that Jacob's name has not been lost in the debris of human history, nor has it been forgotten, as have so many other names. Incredibly, it is forever linked with God. His story is an integral part of the history of divine redemption. This book is about the power of God to transform a human life.

Jacob's story is our story.

www.ingramcontent.com/pod-product-compliance
Lightning Source LLC
Chambersburg PA
CBHW031534040426

42445CB00010B/535